Hobson's Choice

Harold Brighouse

Guide written by
John Mahoney

Charles Letts & Co Ltd
London, Edinburgh & New York

First published 1988
by Charles Letts & Co Ltd
Diary House, Borough Road, London SE1 1DW

Illustrations: Betty Eberl

The author and publishers are grateful to
Samuel French Ltd for permission to quote
extracts from *Hobson's Choice* by Harold Brighouse.
Samuel French Ltd control amateur
performing rights in the play.

This series of literature guides has been conceived and developed by John Mahoney
and Stewart Martin.

John Mahoney has taught English for twenty years. He has been head of the English
department in three schools and has wide experience of preparing students at all levels
for most examination boards. He has worked both in the UK and North America
producing educational books and computer software on English language and literature.
He is married with three children and lives in Worcestershire.

Stewart Martin is an Honours graduate of Lancaster University, where he read English
and Sociology. He has worked both in the UK and abroad as a writer, a teacher, and an
educational consultant. He is married with three children, and is currently deputy
headmaster at Ossett School in West Yorkshire.

British Library Cataloguing in Publication Data
Mahoney, John
Hobson's choice : Harold Brighouse : guide.
—(Guides to literature).
1. Drama in English. Brighouse, Harold,
1882-1958. Hobson's choice. Study outlines
I. Title   II. Martin, Stewart   III. Brighouse
Harold, *1882-1958*   IV. Series
822'.912

ISBN 0 85097 845 9

Printed and bound in Great Britain by
Charles Letts (Scotland) Ltd

Contents

To the student

This study companion to your English literature text acts as a guide to the novel or play being studied. It suggests ways in which you can explore content and context, and focuses your attention on those matters which will lead to an understanding, appreciative and sensitive response to the work of literature being studied.

Whilst covering all those aspects dealt with in the traditional-style study aid, more importantly, it is a flexible companion to study, enabling you to organize the patterns of study and priorities which reflect your particular needs at any given moment.

Whilst in many places descriptive, it is never prescriptive, always encouraging a sensitive personal response to a work of literature, rather than the shallow repetition of others' opinions. Such objectives have always been those of the good teacher, and have always assisted the student to gain high grades in examinations in English literature. These same factors are also relevant to students who are doing coursework in English literature for the purposes of continual assessment.

The major part of this guide is the 'Commentary' where you will find a detailed commentary and analysis of all the important things you should know and study for your examination. There is also a section giving practical help on how to study a set text, write the type of essay that will gain high marks, prepare coursework and a guide to sitting examinations.

Used sensibly, this guide will be invaluable in your studies and help ensure your success in the course.

The illustrations are an attempt to interpret the author's intentions with regard to set design. When you have read the play, study the designs with a view to deciding how the actors would place themselves on stage, and whether these designs might help or hinder the 'movement' of the play. Also try to decide to what extent you feel the character illustrations accurately reflect Willie Mossop, etc.

Harold Brighouse

Harold Brighouse was born near Manchester, in July 1882 (*Hobson's Choice* is set in the year 1880). His mother was a teacher and his father was in the cotton business.

He left school in 1899, at the age of seventeen; he had not been a keen student. However, he was an enthusiastic play-goer, and spent many evenings at the theatre, whilst working for a textile firm in Manchester.

In 1902 he was sent to his firm's branch in London. He again spent much time at the theatre. Apart from attending the theatre, his spare time was spent in writing. He was a member of what became known as the 'Manchester School' of dramatists, many of their plays being based on ordinary folk and situations, as is *Hobson's Choice*.

He wrote numerous plays, and also contributed articles to the *Manchester Guardian*. However, his only work to gain any sort of long-lasting fame is *Hobson's Choice*.

He did not marry, and died in 1958. His autobiography, *What I have had*, was published in 1952.

Understanding Hobson's Choice
An exploration of the major topics and themes in the play

No attempt is made here to be totally comprehensive. You are urged to use this book as a springboard into the text – the true subject of your study. However, we hope to provide you with some of those questions and opinions which are an important adjunct to developing a personal and sensitive investigation of, and response to, a text. We attempt to provide means by which you can read your text with sensitivity to what is happening in its pages, and enjoy the work of literature as a whole. To achieve the latter, it is important to look closely at its constituent parts, before finally 'stepping back', as it were, to admire the whole. Do remember, though, to read your text first, so as to gain an overview of what it is you are studying.

Ambition and money

Recall that this play, though first produced in 1915, is set in Salford, Lancashire, in 1880. At that time, the Victorian values of self-help and independence would have been very much to the fore, and we see in the main characters a reflection of those values, in their determination to 'better' themselves. Would you agree that ambition necessarily involves the acquisition of money? Can we see any occasion in the play when the characters desire something that is not tied in some way to financial considerations? Bear this in mind when you consider some of these other themes, such as love and marriage, choice, and so on.

It seems that Hobson was a self-made man, proud of his own position, and however much he might at heart have recognized the importance of Willie and Maggie in his success, in no way would he admit it. His remaining ambitions seem to centre around the satisfaction of his personal needs – chiefly in the form of drink. Does he have any other ambitions at all?

Initially, Willie's ambition was untapped. With Maggie's decision to marry him, she lets loose and nurtures the ability and ambition that had so far been prevented from surfacing. What evidence is there, near the end of the play, that Willie Mossop had even grander designs than just being partner in Mossop and Hobson? Might Tubby Wadlow have had a hand in teaching Willie any of his skills, and did Tubby have any potential as a craftsman? Was he ever given the opportunity to be ambitious? Is it ever suggested to him that he ought to 'shift' for himself? How does he compare with Willie?

Can you analyse Maggie's ambitions? At the age of thirty she was very nearly beyond the marriageable age (certainly in Victorian eyes), as her father so roughly reminds her. Is she ambitious just to escape spinsterhood? Is hers a selfish ambition, that sees Willie as a means to an end, or is her ambition influenced by her love for Willie as well as her own desire to be married and independent of her father? Do you think her attitude to Willie, and the purposes of her ambition, change during the course of the play?

What is different about the ambitions of Vickey and Alice, and Maggie? They all want to get on in the world, but do they all strive to achieve the same goal?

To what extent is the acquisition of wealth a driving force behind the events and relationships in this play? Is Maggie more concerned, at first, with providing a secure future for herself by a successful business partnership, than with securing a loving and lasting personal relationship? What would you presume are Vickey's and Alice's motives for getting married – apart from a desire not to be 'left on the shelf'? Would they, like Ada and Maggie, ever have considered marrying Willie? If not, why not?

The references made to the necessity of providing a dowry remind us of Victorian values and practices, as do the references that Hobson makes to not paying wages to his daughters, and the minimal wages paid to Tubby and Willie.

Hobson's shop

The trick by which Hobson is caught, the threat of being sued for damages, and Albert's demand for an excessive amount, reflect their very real concern about finance. So too does the attitude of Alice and Vickey when they become suddenly aware that they might be deprived of their 'rightful inheritance' if Maggie moves back into their father's house. Their selfish and acquisitive natures may also be seen in the attitudes they demonstrate when Maggie and Willie remove some broken furniture from the family home.

Choice and conflict

It would be a mistake to see *Hobson's Choice* as being restricted to only one event or character. Whilst the choice that Hobson has to make at the end of the play is related to the title, a number of choices are presented to various other characters in the course of the action. In responding to these challenges, characters are revealed, and we are able to draw conclusions about the various individuals.

When Maggie confronts Willie and Ada with her determination to break up their 'engagement' and marry Willie herself, what do the reactions of Willie and Ada tell us about them? What are their choices in the matter? What is their ability to actually make choices?

What choices face Alice and Vickey? How do they match up to the decisions required of them? For example, consider their reaction to the possibility of Maggie and Willie moving back into the family home and taking over the business. How do they react and why, and what alternative courses of action are open to them? What influences their decisions? Look also at the choices, sometimes unpalatable, forced on their respective suitors/husbands. How does the way they react to the impositions of Maggie help us to judge their characters? What alternative courses of action are open to them?

Our two main male characters, Willie Mossop and Hobson, are presented with the most demanding choices along their respective paths. As we chart the gradual rise of Willie, and the fall of Hobson, each course is signposted by their reaction to crucial decisions.

Finally, we must consider this theme in relation to Maggie. Is it she who acts as the catalyst for virtually all the situations in which the various other characters find themselves? Without Maggie, would there be any choices to make?

Closely tied to the theme of choice, the conflicts that beset the various characters are a fruitful source of investigation. The most obvious conflict in the play is that between Hobson and his three daughters. He clearly has well-formed views about their duties and responsibilities towards him, but those views are rejected by them. His is a self-centred attitude, which sees his offspring as not much more than unpaid labour in his shop.

He is unconcerned about Maggie not being married, as she is invaluable in the shop. However, her own recognition of that value, and his failure to admit it, combined with his unfeeling remarks which write off her chances of being married, are perhaps the root cause of her determination to pursue her own independence, and are the immediate source of conflict between Maggie and her father.

Hobson's wish to marry off his two other daughters, which is immediately abandoned when he realizes they must be provided with a dowry, arises from the purely selfish desire to get them off his hands, no doubt prompted by the fact that they cost him money and contribute but little to the family budget. For their part, as young women with minds of their own, they have every intention of defying his lack of support for their efforts to marry.

The conflict between Hobson and his daughters is clearly evidenced in the opening lines of the play, and continues as an important underlying theme throughout the entire play.

There is also a conflict between Maggie and her sisters, one that she wins. Would you agree that the source of that conflict lies both in Alice and Vickey's selfish concern for their own happiness and future (much like their father's), and in jealousy of Maggie, for her capable handling of both business and parent?

Willie's shop

There is a conflict between Willie and Hobson, but it is one that the presence of Maggie prevents from coming more to the fore. As the main manipulator of events and people (would you agree with this description of her?) she effectively comes between her husband and her father, preventing a swift escalation of events – bear in mind the first scene, when Hobson threatens Willie with his belt. What part does Maggie play in this scene, particularly in relation to the actual conflict between Willie and Hobson?

Note the dispute between Hobson and the Doctor. Hobson's bullying bluff is responded to in kind. What does that scene tell us about both characters? Can you see similarities between them, and might we perhaps see in the Doctor the kind of man that Hobson might have been, but for his self-centredness and drunken ways?

Humour

The central event of this play, lowly worker marrying the boss's daughter and making good, is a fruitful source of ready-made humour and comedy. Add to that mix the deflation of overbearing Hobson, and the plans of his two other daughters, wanting to marry despite him, and humorous opportunities abound.

The major contrasts are between Willie and Hobson. Willie is at first the obvious source of almost slapstick comedy: . . . 'Take that', and Willie ducks, expecting a clout round the ear, but is offered a visiting card; his unwillingness to kiss Maggie; his pleas that his two 'brothers-in-law' should stay longer on his wedding night; the prospect of the wedding feast being cleared so that Maggie could give him his usual reading and writing lessons; these are but a few of many occasions when the audience will have cause for amusement. Would their laughter be at Willie's expense, or would there be an element of sympathy for him? Could you say why this might be so?

The bluff Hobson is almost perfect as a cartoonist's caricature of a self-centred, overbearing parent. Whenever he comes into conflict with his family, he seems bound to lose: the audience senses this and is ready to laugh at his discomfiture. The tribulation he faces over the matter of the 'damages notice' he finds pinned to his chest shows him in perhaps his most vulnerable state. The small and large battles he has and loses: when dinner will be due; shall Maggie marry; whom shall his other daughters marry; the demands of his doctor; these are all occasions which give the audience moments of real amusement. However, how would you define that reaction? Is it the same quality of amusement as we get from the predicaments that Willie finds himself in? If not, can you say why?

Love and marriage

Given that during the course of the play three marriages are arranged, and one frustrated, it is inevitable that the subject is central to the action. At the opening of Act one it swiftly becomes obvious that Alice and Albert are romantically attached. In the middle of that act, Hobson opens his heart to his friend on the problems associated with having three daughters. By the end of that act, we have Maggie breaking up Willie and Ada's relationship and proposing to Willie herself. What do we learn of the attitudes of those three women, Alice, Ada and Maggie, to the men they wish to marry? Is there any evidence that they are in love, in any romantic sense, or do they each just demonstrate a very well-developed sense for the pecuniary advantage that could be gained from the marriages?

Note how in the proposed marriage between Willie and Ada, it was very much a result of Ada's mother manipulating the couple. Could the same be said of Maggie's manipulating Willie into marrying her, and were her intentions and reasons the same as those of Mrs Figgins? Note the attitude of Hobson to marriage and the part he expected to play in arranging his daughters' futures. What is his view of the problems and benefits of marriage and his responsibilities to his daughters in the matter? Do Albert and Fred have any contribution to make to our knowledge of the subject?

Do you think that Willie and Maggie have a true partnership, in every sense of that word? Certainly there was the business partnership of Willie's shoemaking skills and Maggie's sales ability, but was there eventually a personal partnership that went beyond that of business matters? Note the misunderstanding of Willie about Maggie's original partnership proposition – though in what sense was he correct in his view of what she wanted? It is interesting to compare the success Maggie had at the beginning

Hobson's living-room

of the play in breaking up the partnership between Willie and Ada and establishing herself in Ada's place, and her lack of success in imposing her will on the matter of the name for the business partnership between Willie and Hobson.

Did Willie love Ada and did she love him? Was it important for either of them that they should love each other? What views did Willie ever express on the matter of love? Can we learn anything from the relationships between Vickey, Alice, and their suitors about love? Can you identify Maggie's attitude towards romantic love? How important to her was the personal relationship between her and Willie, and would she have wanted to marry had she not been fairly sure of his attitude towards her? For all and any of your responses to these and any other questions, you must be able to point to episodes and incidents which will support your feelings and view of events.

Play technique

As is mentioned elsewhere, you should always remember that the play you read on the page was actually intended to be performed on stage. Such seemingly trivial matters as how an actor makes an entrance, from which side of the stage, the manner in which he bears himself, and the confidence with which he takes on the personality of the character he is playing, are crucial factors in interpreting and conveying the author's and director's intentions.

Reading a play gives us the opportunity to analyse closely the techniques used by the author to set scenes and develop character; to analyse and appreciate structure and consider at leisure such matters as how the characters address each other, and what the stage directions indicate by way of the author's own view of events and characters. None of this is possible in the immediacy of a performance. However, to assist you to a greater awareness of the problems and techniques involved in the actual performance of the play, we comment on many of these matters. You will find them useful for your study of this play, but do also remember that such considerations must equally be borne in mind when you study any play, and from whatever period of our literary history.

Setting – The social and historical context of the play

Do not fail to read the detailed scene descriptions provided by the author. They help ensure the creation of an atmosphere which matches the action of the play. In those descriptions and in the detail of the play itself is a wealth of observation which clearly establishes events in their historical setting.

The description of the shop interior at the beginning of Act one, which acquaints us with the physical surroundings, is swiftly built upon in the ensuing conversations which provide further evidence of the period of time in which the play is set. Note the fact that shoes are made on the premises – unlike any shop we are likely to be acquainted with today; the references to the large trade in clogs; talk of 'carriage trade' (do you understand what it means?); the method of bookkeeping, the references to a room as the 'parlour' and the use of the term 'hand-cart'. These are all fairly minor references, but in the course of the play these and many like them are a major factor in creating the correct sense of atmosphere.

As well as the purely practical points remarked upon in the previous paragraph, there are many aspects of personal relationships which reinforce that sense of place and time of the play's setting. Quite obviously Victorian values, concerns and practices are indicated by the various attitudes expressed towards the subject of marriage, but there are many other examples which assist us in becoming aware of the social atmosphere of the time. The polite form of address between Alice and Albert is perhaps the very first indication of a different time and society from the one we know. The reference to the girls' bustles; Hobson's attitude towards his workers and his act of 'taking a belt' to Willie; the humble attitude adopted by Willie and Tubby towards their master; the slate on which Willie learns to write; the Victorian attitude as to who was 'boss' in the house – although do be aware that in this play it would seem this position has been taken over somewhat by the women; the social distinctions drawn between 'trade' and 'profession' – though even today, we can see considerable evidence that such distinctions still abound and colour attitudes; the play is liberally peppered with such social references and you should be aware of them and of what they are contributing to the action and atmosphere of the play.

Structure

The play's action divides evenly between the various acts, and at the end of Act three, with all three girls married and Willie and Maggie's business prospering, it would seem that the play's concerns have been nicely drawn to their conclusion and all loose ends neatly tied. However, such a view would fail to take into account the central matter of the play's title, *Hobson's Choice*. The bullying and bluster of Hobson have been frustrated, but in Act four he is first confronted by a man determined to affect the course of Hobson's life as he thought to determine his daughters' lives, and also that of Willie. The ensuing choices which first the Doctor, then Maggie and finally Willie present Hobson with firmly bring us back to the play's title and central concern.

It is a play with the plotting and planning of Maggie at its centre, as she successfully manipulates those around her – for their good, and for her own. It is also a play about the development of Willie's potential, but you should not forget that the downfall of Hobson is central to the structure and action. Just as he thought to present his daughters and Willie with 'Hobson's choices' at the beginning of the play, choices which they manage to 'escape', so he too is presented with choices, which he does not escape.

Apart from these central concerns that are the backbone of the play, a whole wealth of minor detail supports the main events. For example, Mrs Hepworth is important in ensuring that Willie is brought to our attention as an expert shoemaker, and her admiration for his skills and Maggie's business acumen help prepare us for the news that she has provided the capital which sets Willie and Maggie up in business.

The whole action of the play largely comprises a series of clashes of will, and the resolution of those clashes. The first one between Maggie and Albert, and the next between Hobson and his daughters prepare us for the strength of Maggie's action in calmly dismissing Ada and supplanting her in Willie's affections. Note those other clashes which mark the course and development of the play, and widen our knowledge of character.

It is also interesting to note how the end of each act marks a definite stage in Willie's and Maggie's growing awareness of each other. At the end of Act one, Willie kisses Maggie in angry defiance of Hobson, but is unresponsive to her act of putting her arms around his neck. At the end of Act two, Willie does not have to be provoked into a response to Maggie, he freely admits that she is 'growing on him' and it is Maggie who stands back, as it were, wanting to gain reassurance that he enters the marriage willingly. By the end of Act three, Willie is again unsure of himself and Maggie decisive. Her action of leading him to bed by the ear leaves us in no doubt as to her determination to be married. Act four, with its 'Eh, lad!' from Maggie, and 'Eh, lass!' from Willie, provides a beautifully balanced ending, with both Willie and Maggie in accord.

Analysis chart

	Salford in 1880					One month later			The same day			One year later			
Act	1					2			3			4			
	Albert buys some boots	Hobson confronts his daughters	Mrs Hepworth, Willie and Jim Heeler	Maggie, Willie and Ada	Reactions to Maggie and Willie's engagement	Alice and Vickey 'run' the business	Maggie and Willie visit Hobson's shop	The writ against Hobson	Wedding celebrations	Hobson joins the wedding celebrations	Vickey and Alice say goodbye	Tubby, Jim Heeler and Hobson	Hobson and Dr MacFarlane	Hobson is visited by his daughters	Willie takes over
Comment no.	1	27	45	83	123	138	149	177	184	200	232	239	250	262	275
Characters Hobson	●	●	●	●	●	●	●			●		●	●	●	●
Maggie	●	●	●	●	●	●	●	●	●	●	●			●	●
Alice	●	●			●	●	●				●			●	●
Vickey	●	●			●	●	●				●			●	●
Willie	●		●	●	●		●	●	●	●	●				●
Albert	●	●			●			●	●	●					
Freddy							●		●						
Mrs Hepworth			●						●		●				
Dr MacFarlane													●		
Tubby			●			●	●	●				●			
Ada				●											
Jim Heeler			●									●			
Themes Ambition and money	●	●	●	●		●	●		●	●	●	●	●	●	●
Choice and conflict	●	●	●	●	●	●	●	●	●	●		●	●	●	●
Humour	●		●	●			●	●	●	●		●	●		
Love and marriage	●	●	●	●	●	●	●	●	●					●	●
Play technique	●	●	●	●	●	●			●	●		●	●		●
Setting	●	●	●			●	●	●	●			●			●
Structure	●	●	●	●	●	●	●	●	●	●	●	●	●	●	●
Act	1					2			3			4			
Page in commentary	20	24	27	33	38	42	43	47	50	52	56	58	59	61	63

Finding your way around the commentary

Each page of the commentary gives the following information:

1 A quotation from the start of each paragraph on which a comment is made, or act/scene or line numbers plus a quotation, so that you can easily locate the right place in your text.

2 A series of comments, explaining, interpreting, and drawing your attention to important incidents, characters and aspects of the text.

3 For each comment, headings to indicate the important characters, themes, and ideas dealt with in the comment.

4 For each heading, a note of the comment numbers in this guide where the previous or next comment dealing with that heading occurred.

Thus you can use this commentary section in a number of ways.

1 Turn to that part of the commentary dealing with the chapter/act you are perhaps revising for a class discussion or essay. Read through the comments in sequence, referring all the time to the text, which you should have open before you. The comments will direct your attention to all the important things of which you should take note.

2 Take a single character or topic from the list on page 18. Note the comment number next to it. Turn to that comment in this guide, where you will find the first of a number of comments on your chosen topic. Study it, and the appropriate part of your text to which it will direct you. Note the comment number in this guide where the next comment for your topic occurs and turn to it when you are ready. Thus, you can follow one topic right through your text. If you have an essay to write on a particular character or theme just follow the path through this guide and you will soon find everything you need to know!

3 A number of relevant relationships between characters and topics are listed on page 18. To follow these relationships throughout your text, turn to the comment indicated. As the previous and next comment are printed at the side of each page in the commentary, it is a simple matter to flick through the pages to find the previous or next occurrence of the relationship in which you are interested.

For example, you may want to examine in depth the theme of choice and conflict. Turning to the topic list, you will find that this theme first occurs in comment 6. On turning to comment 6 you will discover a zero (0) in the place of the previous reference (because this is the first time that it has occurred) and the number 12 for the next reference. You now turn to comment 12 and find that the previous comment number is 6 (from where you have just been looking) and that the next reference is to comment 13, and so on throughout the text.

You may also wish to trace the relationship between Maggie and Willie throughout the play. From the relationships list, you are directed to comment 26. This is the first time that both Maggie and Willie are discussed together, and you will find that two different comment numbers are given for the characters under examination – numbers 30 and 54. This is because each character is traced separately as well as together and you will have to continue tracing them separately until you finally come to comment 96 – the next occasion on which both Maggie and Willie are discussed.

Comment number

Quote from play

Previous appearance in guide

Character or idea under discussion

6 VICKEY: He'll need reviving.
Would you agree that there is a degree of disrespect, and perhaps anger, in their comments about Hobson's behaviour? Their remarks are the first indication of the unhappy state of affairs that exists between him and his daughters. It is a theme that will be much developed in the play.

4/27	Hobson
0/34	Vickey
0/12	Choice and conflict
5/8	Play technique

Next appearance in guide

Commentary

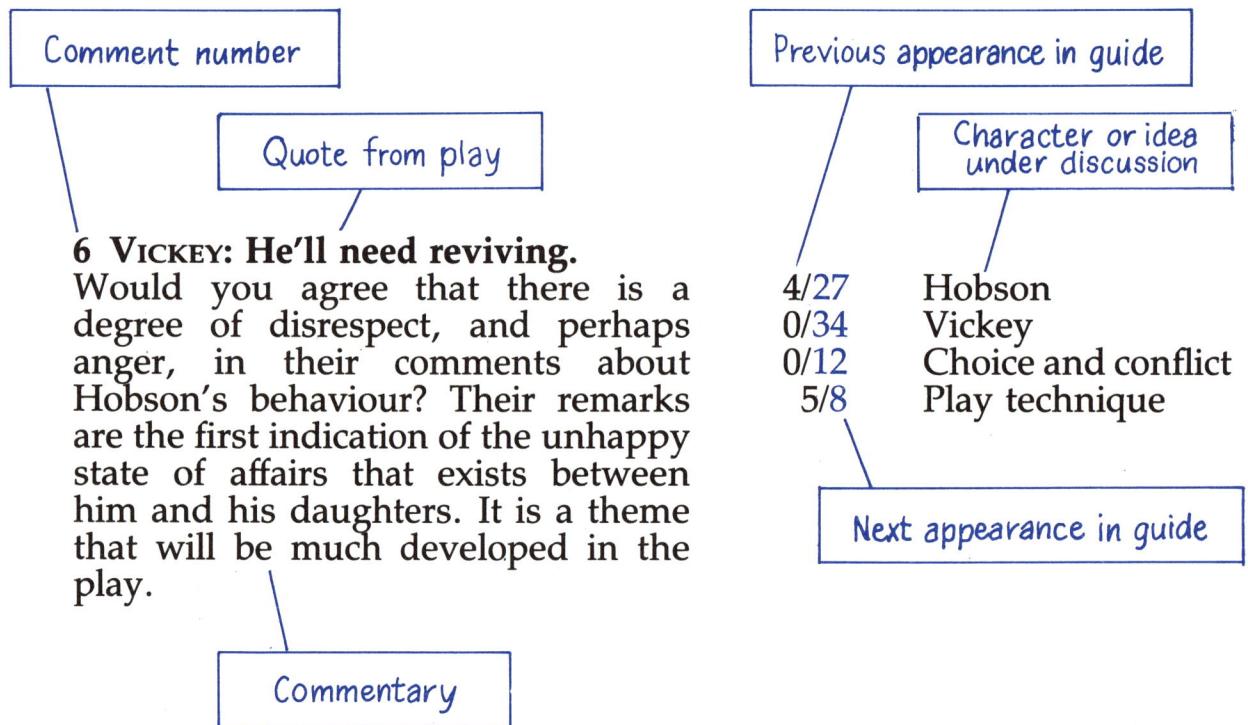

Single topics:

	Comment no:		Comment no:
Hobson	4	Ambition and money	21
Maggie	5	Choice and conflict	6
Alice	4	Humour	15
Vickey	6		
		Love and marriage	2
Willie	26	Play technique	1
Albert	8		
Freddy	149	Setting	1
		Structure	2
Mrs Hepworth	45		
Dr MacFarlane	250		
Tubby	52		
Ada	103		
Jim Heeler	66		

Relationships:

			Comment no:
Maggie	and	Willie	26
	and	Hobson	30
	and	Alice	7
	and	Vickey	172
	and	Ambition and money	21
	and	Love and marriage	20
Willie	and	Hobson	96
	and	Ambition and money	87
	and	Love and marriage	96
Hobson	and	Choice and conflict	6

Commentary

Act One

Salford in 1880

Act 1

1 *The Scene represents the interior . . .*
The detailed description of the stage set, with such comments as *'The business is prosperous'*, *'dingy but business-like'*, *'little stock'* and *'clogs figure prominently'* assists in creating an atmosphere for the ensuing action. Note the scene description also includes practical, essential physical detail: gas brackets, cane chairs and the placing of windows, doors etc.

It is, of course, a matter for the set designer and director of the play to translate the author's directions into an actual stage set. If you get a chance to see the play in performance, try to assess how far you feel those stage directions have been successfully translated into the set. The degree of success achieved is important in the support it gives to the words and events of the play. For example, when you are familiar with the play, try to imagine it being set on a bare stage with only a table and chairs, and perhaps a few boxes for props. How would the words and actions of the characters 'stand up' without the support of the detailed stage set as sketched by the author?

You should always remember, whilst you are studying a play text, that the text was intended to be performed, live, on a real stage and in front of an audience. It is easy to lose sight of that fact when your immediate horizons are bounded by the four walls of a classroom. As you read the text, always try to visualize it as happening in front of you. It takes only a small leap of imagination and a willingness to immerse yourself in Willie and Maggie's world, for the text to begin to come alive.

0/2	Play technique
0/3	Setting

2 *Sitting behind the counter . . .*
Reference to the ages of the three girls is important. When we learn that they are all unmarried we are led to speculate about some of the problems that might arise, especially for Maggie, the eldest. It is the first hint that the theme of marriage will be an important factor in the play and also a major structural link throughout it.

How might you select actresses to convey the age differences between Maggie and her sisters as indicated in the stage directions? It would not be an easy task. Would it be necessary to emphasize the difference by choosing a markedly older-looking actress for Maggie, or would the age gap come across through the words and actions of the actresses involved? Is the disparity of ages actually important?

0/20	Love and marriage
1/5	Play technique
0/9	Structure

3 *Sitting behind the counter . . .*
Picture a modern shoe shop. Can you imagine two of the young assistants reading and knitting? Note the style of dress; such severe modes were typical of the period.

1/10	Setting

4 Alice: **Oh, it's you. . . .**
Through the first lines of the play we are swiftly acquainted with aspects of the father's character: his lateness in getting up, the reference to the Masons' meeting, and the need for him to be 'revived', all suggest a certain lack of sobriety on his part.

Alice's comment that she hoped her father was going out, makes us wonder why, and prepares us for the arrival of Albert.

0/7	Alice
0/6	Hobson

5 MAGGIE: It isn't. . . .

The dominance of Maggie is suggested both by the fact that she arrives last, and thus has to make an 'entrance', and also by her sitting at a desk, obviously engaged with the shop accounts. From the actress's point of view, the way in which that entrance is made and the brevity, almost sharpness of her replies to Alice's questions, would be an important element in creating for the audience an impression of what sort of person she is.

0/7 Maggie
2/6 Play technique

6 VICKEY: He'll need reviving.

Would you agree that there is a degree of disrespect, and perhaps anger, in their comments about Hobson's behaviour? Their remarks are the first indication of the unhappy state of affairs that exists between him and his daughters. It is a theme that will be much developed in the play.

Vickey's comment is rather acid. She was described as being very pretty, is she perhaps also rather nasty? You will have to make your judgement on this matter when you have more evidence from reading further into the text, but it is a point worth bearing in mind. Of course, it may well be that her comment is both accurate and appropriate.

How might an actress give different emphasis to her words to convey a variety of shades of meaning and feeling? What would dictate the emphasis that ought to be used?

4/27 Hobson
0/34 Vickey
0/12 Choice and conflict
5/8 Play technique

7 ALICE: Yes I am, . . .

Do you detect a certain abrasiveness in Alice's tone? Might it be that she is used to having difficulty in meeting Albert in private? For one who is so obviously anxious about the arrival of her visitor, she is not very forthcoming when he does arrive. Or is it perhaps that Maggie is excessively domineering?

4/14 Alice
5/9 Maggie

8 [ALBERT PROSSER enters . . .

Note the description of Albert in these stage directions. Does it give any clue to his character, or is that yet to be established? Entrances and exits of characters are very important, particularly the former. When we first see a character we almost invariably make a judgement about them—but not always wisely or correctly.

An actor, if he is to be successful, must actually feel himself to be the character being played. He will want to establish the character's identity so the audience can react. That desire will be especially relevant when he makes his first entrance—why?

0/9 Albert
6/11 Play technique

9 [ALBERT PROSSER enters . . .

The entrance of Albert brings the first scene, with its hints of drunkenness and conflicts, to a close. We are now to see the emergence of Maggie, demonstrating a very strong and determined character.

What does the following scene say of Albert? Note how it is structured, with Albert first manoeuvred into buying a pair of boot laces (is it the first time this has happened?), then new boots, and finally the repair of his old ones. Apart from anything else, we see the expertise of Maggie the salesgirl at work. It will come as no surprise when she makes a success of her partnership with Willie, nor will we be surprised to learn of her importance to Hobson in this shop.

8/11 Albert
7/11 Maggie
2/19 Structure

10 ALBERT: Good morning, . . .
The social conventions of the time are suggested by their greeting. How might this contrast with the way a man of twenty-six might greet his twenty-three year old girlfriend today?

3/28	Setting

11 ALBERT: Oh! [*He turns* . . .
Does it say much for the strength of his character and affection for Alice, that he makes straight for the door on hearing the news that 'Father's not gone out yet'? He is obviously frightened of the man, despite the fact that he is the son of an established solicitor, which presumably ought to have given him a degree of self-sufficiency and confidence.

As you read the play, do look to see if Albert, and any of the other characters, change at all. Or is it that we just learn more and more about them, and they are no different at the end of the play – neither better nor worse, than they have always been? In this context, it is essential to be able to chart the changes in Willie, Hobson and Maggie.

As suggested before in another context, the way in which the actor plays this attempted exit, and the manner of Maggie's speedy interception of him, will be important in conveying impressions of their characters.

9/12	Albert
9/13	Maggie
8/15	Play technique

12 ALBERT: Eights. I've got . . .
In just a few lines, Maggie has persuaded Albert to buy a pair of shoelaces. He could have refused: after all, it was obvious he had only come to see Alice.

What does the reference he makes to his small feet, his simpering, and the foolish question suggest to you about his character? His inability to determine his own course of action in such simple matters says much about the man.

11/13	Albert
6/13	Choice and conflict

13 [MAGGIE *is on her knees* . . .
The second stage in this short scene is now begun. Having forcefully directed Albert into a chair, Maggie proceeds to sell him a pair of boots. This takes rather longer than the sale of the laces, and he gets ample opportunity to refuse – what use does he make of those opportunities?

12/15	Albert
11/14	Maggie
12/14	Choice and conflict

14 ALICE [*moving down a little*] . . .
This very brief exchange between Alice and Maggie hints at a certain animosity between the two sisters. Is Maggie just being a good saleswoman, or is she also deliberately trying to annoy Alice? Does she really need to wonder why Albert comes in so frequently?

7/21	Alice
13/15	Maggie
13/16	Choice and conflict

15 MAGGIE: Do you get through . . .
Note the sarcasm of 'You must be strong'. There is obviously a contrast here between the word 'strong' and Albert's simpering. Is the audience being invited to laugh at Albert, and thus to side with Maggie?

The picture of Albert keeping a little stock of laces in case of accidents perhaps suggests a rather effeminate character, or is this being unfair to women? Does the picture sit well with the reference to his 'simpering'? You might like to consider whether Albert is being a trifle sarcastic, here. If

13/16	Albert
14/17	Maggie
0/18	Humour
11/17	Play technique

Maggie always treats him like this, then one can well imagine he does have a stock of laces!

16 ALBERT: Oh, no, I really . . .
Despite his protest that he does not wish to buy new boots, Maggie ignores him and proceeds with her sale. Does he have any choice in the matter?

15/18 Albert
14/20 Choice and conflict

17 MAGGIE [*pushing him*]. . . .
This is not the first time that Maggie has pushed Albert. The forcefulness of her character frequently finds expression in physical contact with those around her. As you read the play, look for other instances of this. How might an actress use, and misuse, these physical contacts?

15/18 Maggie
15/27 Play technique

18 ALBERT: A pound! . . .
In 1880 one pound would have been a goodly sum. Albert hasn't actually said he will take the boots yet, but already Maggie has moved on to the subject of which laces he will want for them. Is part of her success as a person and saleswoman the speed, as well as the determination, with which she executes her plans?

Note the sarcastic reference to his strength and his destruction of so many other pairs of laces. Does Maggie actively dislike Albert?

16/20 Albert
17/19 Maggie
15/48 Humour

19 MAGGIE: Very well, . . .
The first two stages in Albert's humiliation at the hands of Maggie have been completed. However, not content with her success, she moves on to a third stage, the mending of Albert's old boots.

18/20 Maggie
9/26 Structure

20 MAGGIE: It's not wasted. . . .
Albert's gasp and his comment, 'if anyone had . . . crazy' is a very weak response to what has just happened to him. Do you think he didn't want to refuse, for fear of embarrassing Alice, or is he just a very weak character? Note how Maggie shows him the door and neither he nor Alice protests. (Who else does Maggie later 'show the door' to?)

Can we reach any conclusions from this meeting with Albert as to the strength of his and Alice's personalities, and of their love for each other?

Are the characters manipulated by Maggie just very weak, or is it that she is unusually forceful, opinionated and overbearing – much like her father probably was, and partly still is?

18/35 Albert
19/21 Maggie
16/23 Choice and conflict
2/22 Love and marriage

21 ALICE: Maggie, we know . . .
Why didn't Alice speak up before? Most people find it personally embarrassing to speak out in any public situation, but is this sufficient reason for Alice to have stayed quiet? Look for evidence in the next few lines as to why Maggie acted like this.

The reference to Maggie being a 'pushing sales-woman' is the first hint we get of her ambitious nature. It is a topic which will shortly find even clearer expression.

14/23 Alice
20/22 Maggie
0/36 Ambition and money

22 MAGGIE [*returning to . . .*

The frequent visits of Albert to the shop have obviously annoyed Maggie. Is it just that her sales instinct is offended by having a potential customer in the shop yet not selling anything, or does she perhaps find the frequent visits of her sister's young man a source of annoyance and frustration at her own lack of prospects in that area?

21/23	Maggie
20/24	Love and marriage

23 MAGGIE: I know it's time . . .

It would seem that Maggie has sold Albert many a pair of laces in the past! She refers to his making 'sheep's eyes' at Alice, and spurs Alice into a fairly spirited defence.

21/25	Alice
22/24	Maggie
20/24	Choice and conflict

24 ALICE: It's all very well for . . .

Alice's reference to Maggie as an old maid foreshadows the same response that her father will make. It would seem that there is an undercurrent of antagonism, and perhaps it is this that prompts Maggie to take firm action over the matter.

23/26	Maggie
23/29	Choice and conflict
22/25	Love and marriage

25 ALICE: Courting must come first.

It would seem that as far as Alice is concerned, the trappings of marriage are very important. Left to herself and Albert, do you think they would ever get married, especially in view of the influence their father wields over two of his daughters? How important do you feel the courting is, given the strained circumstances under which it is apparently taking place?

23/38	Alice
24/42	Love and marriage

26 MAGGIE: It needn't. . . .

Maggie's attitude towards courting is very clearly expressed. Is she right? Does the answer to this question depend very much upon the circumstances?

Note how this reference to useless glitter foreshadows her choice of wedding ring. Does Willie share her view on this?

The final comment about glitter marks the end of the two major scene divisions so far. The first introduced us to Maggie and her sisters, and the second explored in some detail the character of Albert and his relationship with Alice, and introduced the topic of love and marriage. What did we learn along the way about the characters of the three girls?

References having been made to Hobson, it is now the time for him to be introduced, the audience's appetite having been suitably whetted.

24/30	Maggie
0/54	Willie
19/35	Structure

27 [HENRY HORATIO HOBSON *enters . . .*

The description of Hobson should immediately alert us to the possibility of a clash of wills with Maggie. It has previously been suggested that perhaps she is much like her father: a sure recipe for conflict.

The description of Hobson leaves us in little doubt as to how he views his responsibilities as a parent. The phrase 'parent of the period' ought to suggest an insensitivity to his daughters' needs, such as will be borne out by the ensuing events. What else might it suggest to us? How ought the actor playing this character to bear himself? How would you visualize his physical presence? What do you think is meant by the phrase 'His clothes are bought to wear'?

6/28	Hobson
17/29	Play technique

28 MAGGIE: Yes, father. Don't . . .
Just as Maggie begins this scene with a reminder about dinner, so will it end. She is nothing if not consistent and determined.

Despite the description of Hobson as being a 'parent of the period', the evidence of these remarks from his daughters would suggest that he does not rule quite so firmly in his own house.

27/29	Hobson
10/32	Setting

29 HOBSON [*putting his hat* . . .
The critical remarks of his daughters prompt Hobson to attempt a stand against them. Why does he sit in the armchair at this point? Does it represent an attitude of authority? Is it a commanding position from which to address his daughters? Does he feel the need of its support?

Do you find his 'I won't have it' a bit weak? How might an actor speak these lines to show Hobson in different lights?

Is there evidence here to suggest that there has been a state of conflict between him and his daughters for some time now?

28/30	Hobson
24/30	Choice and conflict
27/32	Play technique

30 MAGGIE: I expect Mr Heeler's . . .
The calmness with which Maggie presumably makes this remark, studiously ignoring her father's last speech, may be calculated to annoy him – would you agree?

29/31	Hobson
26/31	Maggie
29/33	Choice and conflict

31 HOBSON: He can go . . .
Notice the length of Hobson's speeches. Generally they are in marked contrast to the short sentences spoken by most other characters, with the major exception of Maggie. To what extent do you think the wordy sentences of Hobson reflect aspects of his character? Is he in love with the sound of his own voice? Look for evidence of this later in the play.

Are Maggie's longish speeches similar to her father's, or is there more purpose to their content?

30/32	Hobson
30/36	Maggie

32 HOBSON: He can go . . .
The reference to the girls' mother being dead helps to clarify why this situation might have arisen. Whilst the father would normally be assumed to be the master in the Victorian household, no doubt the disciplining of daughters would be the wife's province. It is perhaps understandable that Hobson is a bit out of his depth with three unmarried daughters on his hands. Should we feel any sympathy for him?

Could the play be realistically staged so as to present Hobson as a sympathetic figure? What sort of problems would this create for the director?

31/33	Hobson
29/62	Play technique
28/35	Setting

33 HOBSON: I'm talking now, . . .
Ought it to have been necessary for him to state 'you'll none rule me'? Later he will demonstrate how he is prepared to rule Willie, but he is not sure of himself when it comes to his daughters.

32/35	Hobson
30/34	Choice and conflict

34 HOBSON: Yes, you are. . . .
So far Vickey has taken little part in the proceedings, being content, it seems, to read her book and throw in the odd remark. Do you think she is really interested in the book or is it merely a pretence which attempts to place her

6/37	Vickey
33/35	Choice and conflict

above and beyond the clashes of personality which are occurring around her? Does she contribute to these clashes in any way?

35 HOBSON: Yes, you are. . . .
Is his condemnation of lawyers a general dislike of the profession, or directed more at Albert, the son of a solicitor? In Victorian days lawyers had an unenviable reputation – Charles Dickens' *Bleak House* had much to say about lawyers who made a fat profit out of their practice, to the detriment and often bankruptcy of their clients.

Note how this hatred of lawyers is used later in the story by the author, when Hobson is threatened with the possibility of action being taken against him in the courts.

20/24	Albert
33/36	Hobson
34/40	Choice and conflict
32/37	Setting
26/45	Structure

36 HOBSON: I give and . . .
The introduction by Hobson of the subject of money is instantly regretted, and he swiftly changes the subject. Does he feel he is on weak ground here? If so, why?

Maggie is very quick to pick him up with her request that he tells them how much a week he gives them. Is this yet more evidence of Maggie's growing sense of grievance and dissatisfaction with the life she is leading in the Hobson household?

35/38	Hobson
31/44	Maggie
21/41	Ambition and money

37 HOBSON: Vickey, you're pretty, . . .
Does it seem that the prettiness of Vickey grates somewhat on Hobson. Has he mentioned it before?

Note the reference to lying 'like a gas-meter'. It is not a term in use today, but one can imagine that in the early days of gas being installed into houses, some, perhaps many, of the private companies involved would not have been too bothered about the accuracy of their meters – as long as any mistakes were in their favour.

34/38	Vickey
35/39	Setting

38 HOBSON: Vickey, you're pretty, . . .
He turns the attack to the matter of their dress, because he feels on fairly safe ground. After all, he has actually given them money to spend on dresses.

Note how Maggie is not included in his condemnation of their mode of dress and display of themselves around the town. What can we learn from his remarks both about himself and his habits, and the characters and attitudes of two of his daughters?

25/124	Alice
36/41	Hobson
37/125	Vickey

39 VICKEY: Do you want . . .
The reference to mill girls and 'French Madams' helps place the play in the context of the time. It also shows a degree of snobbishness on the part of Vickey and Alice.

37/47	Setting

40 HOBSON: Then I've a choice . . .
Is this the first of Hobson's choices that he imposes on those around him? What exactly is a 'Hobson's choice'? The original Hobson was Thomas Hobson of Cambridgeshire (1544?–1631). He was a carrier who insisted on his customers hiring his horses each in its proper turn, irrespective of its

35/43	Choice and conflict

condition or suitability. A simple expression of Hobson's choice is found in the phrase 'like it or lump it', in other words no choice at all.

41 HOBSON: Then I've a choice . . .
The bullying tone of Hobson well suits his words. He knows the impossibility of girls thrown out of house and home being able to find themselves husbands, particularly in Victorian days. His threat to find a pair of husbands for them is empty, but it would probably solve a major problem for him: two girls who contribute nothing much to his business but who help eat its profits!

| 38/46 | Hobson |
| 36/61 | Ambition and money |

42 HOBSON: You? [*He turns* . . .
The callous and brutal way in which he addresses Maggie is calculated to turn the audience against him. Perhaps by now some might have sympathized with the man, given his two shrewish daughters and the third bossy, determined one. (Is that a reasonable picture of the three, and can you advance reasons and evidence for your answer?) However, the subject of Maggie's marriageability, whilst a joke for Hobson and his other daughters, is a very serious matter for Maggie. Quite obviously, the evidence that she is seriously concerned about this matter is building up, and we should not be too surprised when she shortly accosts Willie on the subject.

| 25/43 | Love and marriage |

What do you think she is concerned about at the moment – not having a sweetheart, or the prospect of being left 'on the shelf'?

43 HOBSON [*facing her*] . . .
The dismissal of Maggie's comment that she is but thirty by the boorish remark that she is 'shelved', coupled with the way he turns from her to address his other two daughters as though she mattered not one bit, must be deeply hurtful to her. It demonstrates the insensitivity of the man, and perhaps helps to explain the determination of Maggie to get her own way, as demonstrated earlier in this act (when?).

| 40/44 | Choice and conflict |
| 42/44 | Love and marriage |

Again, Hobson threatens to marry off his daughters – an attempt at a final routing remark to establish his dominance in the household. Does he succeed?

Do you think Hobson loves his daughters, in any sense at all?

44 MAGGIE: One o'clock . . .
It is a tribute to the strength of Maggie's character that she is able to ignore her father's hurtful and derogatory comments. The calmness with which she then reminds him of the time when dinner will be ready ought to give us pause for thought. Perhaps she has already made up her mind as to the future course of action she will be taking.

36/63	Maggie
43/79	Choice and conflict
43/73	Love and marriage

Has she any real choice in the matter, especially bearing in mind the strength of her character and the insensitivity of her father? How would you judge at this moment the reasons that prompt her to marry Willie?

45 HOBSON: So long as . . .
The arrival of Mrs Hepworth marks another stage in the development of the action. Her presence in the play is structurally important as she provides the means by which Maggie and Willie are able to break away from Hobson and set up on their own.

| 0/50 | Mrs Hepworth |
| 35/50 | Structure |

46 HOBSON: So long as . . .
The decision of Hobson to stay may stem from a variety of causes. Is it because he wishes to re-establish his position as 'master' in his shop and demonstrate his own competence, especially with a wealthy customer (would he have stayed if a poor person had been arriving to buy some clogs?). Or is he just intrigued as to why Mrs Hepworth should be visiting his establishment?

41/48   Hobson

47 HOBSON: So long as . . .
The reference to Mrs Hepworth arriving by carriage should give you a clear clue as to what the phrase 'carriage trade', as shortly used by Jim Heeler, means.

39/48   Setting

48 HOBSON [*kneeling* . . .
A strange and rather ridiculous picture, that of Hobson grovelling around Mrs Hepworth's feet. The stage direction with regard to his controlling his feelings comes before Mrs Hepworth's remark that he looks ridiculous, so they cannot be of anger or embarrassment–or could they? Just what do you suppose were the feelings that he had to control? The text does not make this totally clear and the actor would have to make a decision here as to exactly how this little scene was going to be played. This is an opportunity for humour, at Hobson's expense. Should it be played that way?

46/49   Hobson
18/49   Humour
47/53   Setting

49 HOBSON: They were made . . .
This exchange between Hobson and Mrs Hepworth sets the scene for an amusing interlude of misunderstandings. Is Hobson being deliberately dense, not wanting to admit that he did not know who made the boots, or is he being circumspect in his answer because he is afraid a complaint is about to be delivered?

48/51   Hobson
48/55   Humour

50 MRS HEPWORTH [*to Maggie*] . . .
Mrs Hepworth's comment establishes that she already knows and has some respect for Maggie. This is important, because it helps the audience accept her later action in providing funds for Maggie and Willie's business partnership.

45/56   Mrs Hepworth
45/52   Structure

51 HOBSON: I am responsible . . .
Does Hobson sense that control of the situation is slipping away from him and passing into Maggie's hands?

49/53   Hobson

52 [TUBBY WADLOW *comes up* . . .
Tubby does not play a large part in the play. His appearance here merely acquaints the audience with the fact of his presence, so that no explanation is needed in later scenes when he has a bit more to do. Note his description. Would you say he was nothing more than a drudge for Hobson, and does his appearance confirm this?

0/140   Tubby
50/56   Structure

53 HOBSON: Name of Mossop, . . .
The attitude of Hobson to the possibility of Willie having done something wrong is interesting. It throws light on contemporary attitudes towards low-paid workers. Can you imagine any modern employer of however small a business feeling able to threaten to physically punish his workers–if we are

51/58   Hobson
48/54   Setting

to interpret his words in that way? Would you agree it gives a most unflattering glimpse of the true nature of Hobson?

---

54 [WILLIE MOSSOP *comes up* . . .
The description of Willie is important. It refers not only to his appearance, but also to his background. We learn of his current status, and more importantly, his potential.

26/55	Willie
53/55	Setting

Given the reference to his clothes being in a poorer state than Tubby's, do you think he therefore holds a lesser position in the shop hierarchy?

The reference to a 'brutalized childhood' gives us another hint about the times (though modern society has a lot to answer for in this respect as well). He is not stupid, but perhaps the most telling phrase is 'raw material of a charming man'. Bear it in mind and when you have finished studying the text, try to determine how far Willie has been able to realize the promise contained in that description of his potential.

---

55 MRS HEPWORTH: Take that.
A gentle piece of farce, with Willie misunderstanding the implication of 'Take that'. Does it suggest, however, that in his automatic reaction to the phrase he is familiar with another outcome? Would the audience laugh at Willie here?

54/59	Willie
49/58	Humour
54/61	Setting

---

56 MRS HEPWORTH: Take that.
The receipt of Mrs Hepworth's visiting card is a small, but important structural link in the story. Though we do not witness the event in the play, it provides the means and justification for an approach to be made to Mrs Hepworth when Willie and Maggie set up on their own. It is a minor point, but does indicate the care which the author has taken to ensure there is a logical and believable sequence of events which enables Willie and Maggie to gain their independence.

50/57	Mrs Hepworth
52/59	Structure

---

57 MRS HEPWORTH: Bless the man. . . .
We do not learn much about Mrs Hepworth as a character in the play, except that she helps Willie and Maggie. That fact alone allows us to deduce something about her – what?

56/59	Mrs Hepworth

How do you imagine Hobson would have reacted to someone who could not read his visiting card and was not even sure that it had writing on it? Note Mrs Hepworth's reaction, 'Bless the man.'. The phrase could only have been said in a kindly way, and it does enable us to add just a little more to our appreciation of Mrs Hepworth's character.

---

58 HOBSON [*moving slightly towards her*] . . .
Another misunderstanding. This time, however, it is again Hobson failing to appreciate Mrs Hepworth's remarks, jumping in without thought and so being made to look an idiot. Perhaps he is already beginning to regret his decision to stay behind and greet Mrs Hepworth. So far he has gained nothing but aggravation and humiliation. Being told to hold his tongue, in front of his drudge and three daughters, cannot have been received very well by him. No doubt the audience will have enjoyed his discomfiture, though.

53/65	Hobson
55/62	Humour

---

59 Mrs Hepworth: You'll keep that . . .
The purpose of Willie being given the visiting card is spelt out. The suggestion that he might at some time leave Hobson's employ prepares the audience for some of the events about to happen.

57/65	Mrs Hepworth
55/62	Willie
56/60	Structure

60 Hobson: Oh, he won't . . .
The certainty Hobson expresses, that Willie won't make a change, and Mrs Hepworth's immediate rebuff of that statement helps to prepare the audience for the fact that Willie does eventually leave Hobson's employ.

59/63	Structure

61 Hobson: Oh, he won't . . .
The power of an employer in Victorian times to ensure that an employee could not get another job, if he left against his employer's will, was quite wide: not legally so, but in practice it frequently happened.

Mrs Hepworth's recognition of Willie's value and the fact that Hobson probably underpaid him shows her perception of Willie's potential and confirms the meanness of Hobson. Note how he does not reply, but immediately dismisses Willie.

41/64	Ambition and money
55/67	Setting

62 Mrs Hepworth: He's like a rabbit.
The comment about the way Willie disappeared, allied to the way in which the actor 'plays' the exit, would occasion some humour. The reference to his being like a rabbit also reinforces the mental image we currently have of Willie – an image which is about to change.

59/83	Willie
58/107	Humour
32/66	Play technique

63 Maggie: Can I take . . .
The speed with which Maggie interrupts and tries to gain another order says a great deal about her sense of business acumen. Again, it shows the care with which the author prepares the ground for the future and ensures that the audience will find it easier to accept the sequence of events as they unfold.

44/75	Maggie
60/65	Structure

64 Hobson: Good morning, . . .
Angry at his rebuff, Hobson complains about Mrs Hepworth's praise of Willie. However, it is not just anger that occasions this complaint, but a half-real concern that it might lead Willie to getting a bit 'beyond' himself and perhaps expecting more money, and that would never do for Hobson.

61/76	Ambition and money

65 Hobson: I'll show her. . . .
The pettiness of the man is demonstrated here. Is this just an empty threat, as Maggie's comment would suggest?

The departure of Mrs Hepworth marks another stage in the development of the play. All the main characters have now been introduced, and the major themes which the play deals with have, to a greater or lesser degree, been aired.

Mrs Hepworth does not appear again in the play. However, references and allusions are made to her, and her helpful influence is felt as a major factor in the working out of the main action of the play.

58/69	Hobson
59/188	Mrs Hepworth
63/71	Structure

66 [Enter from the street . . .
Jim Heeler makes but two appearances in the play. You should be aware of
when and under what circumstances, as indeed you should be aware for all
other characters. Here, he acts as a confidant, allowing Hobson to unburden
his mind not only to Jim, but more importantly to the audience. Thus we are
able to make a better judgement as to Hobson's character and subsequent
actions.

0/72	Jim Heeler
62/68	Play technique

67 JIM: You're doing a . . .
The reference to 'carriage trade' was mentioned before in this commentary.
Can you recall the circumstances? It will help you understand what the
phrase means.

61/72	Setting

68 HOBSON: Oh, yes. Mrs . . .
Hobson is quick to take upon himself credit for having Mrs Hepworth as a
customer. How might an actor play this line: dismissively, as though such
customers were nothing unusual in this shop; or perhaps unctuously, with a
rubbing of the hands to suggest the lucrative and successful trade that was
involved? There are undoubtedly other ways – can you imagine any?

66/70	Play technique

69 HOBSON: Why, I've made . . .
What was it that Hobson accused Vickey of earlier? Is he guilty of the same
character failing here?

65/73	Hobson

70 [The girls go out . . .
Can you imagine why the stage directions require Maggie to leave last? Is it
because she is the most important of the three girls, or is it that she hangs
behind, hoping to hear what her father and Heeler are to talk about?

68/106	Play technique

71 HOBSON: They're the trouble. . . .
We have heard some of Alice's and Vickey's complaints against their father,
now it is Hobson's turn to acquaint the audience with what is worrying him.
Have we had any explicit comment from Maggie about her attitudes to her
father?

65/81	Structure

72 JIM: Nay – . . . they mostly . . .
The authority of the Victorian father is described here. Can you imagine a
casual reference to 'leathering' in such a conversation today?

66/76	Jim Heeler
67/78	Setting

73 HOBSON: Ah, Jim, a wife's . . .
Hobson's view of marriage receives a small airing here. It would seem that
he was not master in his own house when Mary was alive; now he is even
less so. Despite all his bullying and blustering ways then, would he seem to
be a coward at heart?

69/74	Hobson
44/77	Love and marriage

74 HOBSON: I'm a talkative man . . .
What evidence, already referred to in this commentary, would support
Hobson's view of himself as a talkative man?

73/75	Hobson

75 HOBSON: I am. [*He turns*] . . .
His comment previously that his daughters consider him to be a windbag, and here that they scorn his wisdom, confirm to the audience what they must have suspected, if not known, all the time: his daughters have lost any respect they might ever have had for him. However, it is also obvious that whilst Alice and Vickey might feel strong enough to argue against him, they still depend on him for food and lodging. Maggie, however, is a different case – in what way?

76 JIM: Then you quit roaring . . .
Jim's simple solution is to get the daughters wed. However, for Hobson this isn't so simple, as he wants them to marry 'temperance' young men: young men who don't drink. Given Hobson's lifestyle, is it likely that he will ever make the acquaintance of such men?

To what extent do you think that Hobson's ambition for his daughters is related to the money he will save as well as the peace he will gain?

77 HOBSON: Vickey and Alice . . .
A crucial comment here from Hobson. In two brief sentences he demonstrates the poverty of his attitude towards his daughters. He is happy to lose Alice and Vickey because they are no help in the shop and thus contribute nothing to his wealth. On the other hand, he wants to keep Maggie because she generates wealth for him. It is a straightforward balance of commercial considerations; morality, ethics, love and affection for family, all have no place in his calculations.

78 HOBSON: . . . Eh? Oh, I'll . . .
Note the antiquated expression about 'getting his hand down' for the money. In *Brewer's Dictionary of Phrase and Fable*, there are some seventy-three colloquial expressions noted which use the image of a hand, but this is not one of them. What would you imagine it means? The context in which the phrase is used ought to give you a clear clue.

79 HOBSON: I've changed my mind. . . .
The swiftness with which Hobson has changed his mind about getting his daughters married says much about the value he puts on his money. His daughters' future happiness is of rather less concern to him.

Note how all the arguments Jim Heeler puts in favour of marriage are made and rejected on economic grounds. He will not save on their keep because they do not eat much and also they work for their keep. He will not save their wages because he does not pay any.

So far as Hobson is concerned, there is no choice to be made. It is 'Hobson's Choice' as soon as he realizes their marrying would cost him money.

80 HOBSON: . . . From the moment . . .
Is there a sense of relief on Hobson's part at the decision he has just made? The worries he has had about the unruliness of his daughters are completely outweighed by the relief he feels at discovering that keeping them at home is saving him money.

He can now depart for the 'Moonraker's' with an easy mind.

Characters and ideas
previous/next comment

74/76 Hobson
63/84 Maggie

75/77 Hobson
72/249 Jim Heeler
64/77 Ambition and money

76/79 Hobson
76/79 Ambition and money
73/79 Love and marriage

72/149 Setting

77/80 Hobson
77/80 Ambition and money
44/110 Choice and conflict
77/84 Love and marriage

79/82 Hobson
79/87 Ambition and money

81 MAGGIE [*remaining by the door*] . . .
The reference to dinner being at one helps to remind the audience both of previous events and the time of the day. The departure of Hobson and Jim Heeler for the 'Moonraker's', leaving just Maggie in the shop, provides the opportunity for the next stage of the play's development – the match between Maggie and Willie.

71/105   Structure

82 HOBSON: Dinner will be when . . .
Is there an air almost of confidence in Hobson's voice in his assertion that 'I'm master here'? Perhaps he is overcome by the happiness he feels at having discovered he is saving money by keeping his daughters at home. In the sense that he is preventing Alice and Vickey from marrying, one supposes that he is master.

Note the irony, however, that having resolved the matter of his daughters' marriage prospects to his satisfaction, Maggie will now take a hand and upset all his plans.

80/85   Hobson

83 MAGGIE: Yes, they're dirty, . . .
The question about who taught Willie highlights the fact that his is a skill which is innate. As such, he perhaps attains even greater dignity, because he relies on no one else for his abilities.

62/87   Willie

84 MAGGIE: Yes, they're dirty, . . .
Note the way she holds and retains his hands in her grasp. She obviously admires his skill, but is there also a hint here that equally she admires the man as well? It is important to examine carefully the relationship between Maggie and Willie and the degree to which she demonstrates any affection for him. It is too easy to assume that the only initial attraction Willie has for Maggie is as a means of escape from her father's household and certain spinsterhood.

75/85   Maggie
79/86   Love and marriage

85 MAGGIE: Hobson's never . . .
An interesting comment from Maggie. It adds a bit more to the information we have about Hobson. What sort of things might we deduce from her remark, about Hobson and her opinion of him?

82/127   Hobson
84/86   Maggie

86 MAGGIE [*dropping his hands*] . . .
How might the actress speak this line about Willie being a 'natural fool'? Would it be said with regret, or a sense of determination to indicate it was a state of affairs she intended to rectify? What would the overall context of the play suggest about how the line should be spoken? (A clue would be the decision that Maggie has already made as to her future with Willie.)

85/88   Maggie
84/93   Love and marriage

87 MAGGIE: When are you . . .
There have already been hints to the audience that Willie could leave Hobson's: can you remember where? Here, Maggie broaches the subject directly, but with disappointing results.

Note how Willie's concern is whether he's given satisfaction, not whether he's gained satisfaction. Do you think he is happy there? Before you judge him as being without ambition or much character, do remember his

83/89   Willie
80/88   Ambition and money

'brutalized childhood', the sense of satisfaction and fulfilment that a craftsman gets from his trade, the sense of 'security' he may well feel at Hobson's, despite the nature of his master. It is very easy to make critical judgements of those seemingly without ambition; you must also bear in mind their circumstances and opportunities.

88 WILLIE: Not me. I've been . . .
The task before Maggie is indicated by Willie's comment here. However, we have already seen how determined she can be. Willie does not know, yet, what's going to hit him.

86/91   Maggie
87/89   Ambition and money

89 WILLIE: Then I'm a . . .
An interesting aspect of Willie's character. He replies with some spirit to Maggie's second reference to his being a fool. Has she annoyed him with her abrasive attitude and comments? Does it suggest there is more to this man than we might at first suspect?

Recall the comment that Willie was 'the raw material of a charming man'. Would loyalty, however misguided, be a characteristic of such a man? Why would you say that Willie's loyalty to Hobson was misguided? Is it really loyalty he feels, or is the word but an empty excuse for his staying put at Hobson's?

87/90   Willie
88/92   Ambition and money

90 WILLIE: I dunno what it is. . . .
Willie doesn't know what keeps him here; does he care?

89/94   Willie

91 MAGGIE: Do you know . . .
Maggie gives utterance to the fact of who keeps the business going. Note her comments about selling the boots. She takes absolutely no credit for selling the boots that Willie makes: 'they sell themselves'. Her contribution is being able to sell the rubbish that other people make. It is a striking piece of honest appraisal, and assists us in making a rounded judgement of Maggie's character.

88/92   Maggie

92 MAGGIE [*stopping him*] . . .
We have witnessed other occasions when Maggie has quite forcefully persuaded others to sit, go, or stay. Here, that determination is very important. If Willie goes, her chances of a future go with him.

91/93   Maggie
89/93   Ambition and money

93 MAGGIE: To invest in. . . .
Might we assume from this that Maggie's only concern is her ambition to run a successful business? Certainly her remark clearly admits of this interpretation. However, in judging her motives, be aware that her monetary ambitions do not necessarily preclude her from having any affection for Willie. What evidence is there for the latter?

92/95   Maggie
92/95   Ambition and money
86/95   Love and marriage

94 WILLIE [*getting up,* . . .
Why should Willie be so relieved that marriage was not involved? Is his remark on almost the next line the clue to his relief?

Marrying the master's daughter has almost the fairy tale touch – especially for the child from a poor and brutalized background. Is there ever a sense of

90/96   Willie

sentimentality in the story of Maggie and Willie's love affair? If not, how does the author avoid such a feeling?

95 MAGGIE: Maybe that's why, . . .
The analysis of Maggie's motives for wanting to marry Willie is helped by this reference to her father. Is it a mixture of business ambition, desire to get away from her father, fear at the thought of spinsterhood, admiration of Willie's skills, the stark contrast in manners and attitudes between Willie and her father, a growing affection for Willie and a realization of what he might become? Does she know a bargain, in every sense of the word, when she sees one?

93/96	Maggie
93/102	Ambition and money
93/96	Love and marriage

96 WILLIE: I am doing. . . .
The openness of Maggie, in the previous lines, when she describes Willie as being her best chance, receives an equally frank reply. Despite recognizing her 'shapely body' and sales expertise, Willie admits he's 'none in love' with her.

This exchange shows both Willie and Maggie in a sympathetic light. Neither is attempting to take advantage of the other, a noticeable contrast with Hobson, who takes advantage not only of his workmen but also of his daughters.

95/97	Maggie
94/98	Willie
95/97	Love and marriage

97 MAGGIE: Wait till you're asked. . . .
Maggie declares what she wants from Willie. It is a straightforward proposition that recognizes there will be problems and that the contract would be for life. It is, then, more than just a business proposition that Maggie is putting to Willie.

96/99	Maggie
96/98	Love and marriage

98 WILLIE: We'd not get much . . .
No fool, Willie immediately points out that marriage without love is not a good foundation for a lasting relationship. An interesting point, bearing in mind that he seems to have agreed to enter into just such a relationship with Ada.

96/100	Willie
97/109	Love and marriage

99 MAGGIE: I've got the love . . .
This exchange where Maggie says she has 'got the love', and if Willie hasn't, they will get along without, adds point to the remark Willie makes that she must be desperate. Is she? Has her behaviour struck you so far as that of one who is desperate to get married? Determined, certainly, but desperate? What do you think, and why?

97/102	Maggie

100 WILLIE: Oh, nay, I'm not. . . .
Despite the shock he has just received, and the determination of Maggie, Willie remains reasonable and equally determined that Maggie shall not have her way. You might like to contrast his attitude to Maggie's pressure with that demonstrated by Albert, earlier in the story. Which has demonstrated the stronger character?

98/101	Willie

101 WILLIE: What makes it . . .
Willie's engagement comes as rather a shock to Maggie. It is an event she had not anticipated. We have already heard Willie's attitude towards the

100/104	Willie

duty of loyalty; is he loyal to Ada, and is that why he turns down Maggie?

102 MAGGIE: The scheming hussy. . . .

Is there any justification for Maggie's comment here, other than annoyance at the frustration of her carefully worked out plans? We can perhaps better understand her attitude if we remember the plans she has built in her mind around her marriage to Willie. Perhaps she is desperate after all?

99/103   Maggie
95/104   Ambition and money

103 MAGGIE: And so shall I. . . .

A good judge of character, Maggie quickly realizes that Ada will be no match for her. Is Willie the 'helpless sort'?

0/106   Ada
102/104   Maggie

104 MAGGIE: And that gives me . . .

Is it such a bad life that Maggie paints for Ada and Willie? Is Willie already a 'contented slave' – of Hobson? Willie says he is not ambitious, but Maggie is determined otherwise. Is there any justification at all for saying she is merely an interfering, self-centred busybody, much like her father?

103/115   Maggie
101/105   Willie
102/120   Ambition and money

105 WILLIE: Aye, so you say. . . .

Are we to assume that Willie is expecting Ada to put up a fight for him? It seems a reasonable assumption. But note how he puts the onus on Ada. He has made his protest and had it rejected by Maggie. Does it show a degree of spinelessness on his part, or loyalty to his bargain with Ada, or a sensible appreciation of the adage 'may the best man (woman) win'?

On cue, Ada enters and marks the beginning of the next stage in the story.

104/108   Willie
81/126   Structure

106 [ADA FIGGINS enters from . . .

To what extent does Ada live down to Maggie's opinion of her? Is her appearance likely to cause the audience to feel pity for her? If so, it is an opinion that they may soon change. You should look for how the author is directing the audience's sympathies according to the direction he wants the plot to go. However, whatever the author's intentions, the audience may well feel differently.

103/107   Ada
70/115   Play technique

107 MAGGIE: I want a word with you. . . .

The immediate injection of humour into this scene, at the expense of Ada as she looks stupidly at Maggie's feet, is enough to prejudice the audience against her. The misunderstanding 'gush' heightens the effect. This is a similar technique to that used when Mrs Hepworth came into the shop earlier in the play.

106/109   Ada
62/112   Humour

108 ADA: Maybe he's not . . .

A new insight into Willie: he is musical – it is only a Jew's harp, but even that is perhaps surprising when we remember his 'brutalized childhood', and the fact that he is 'stunted mentally'. Where were they mentioned?

105/110   Willie

109 ADA: I see the lad . . .

What do you imagine Ada means by love? Is it merely 'want'? And if so, is it any different from what Maggie wants? Are we right to assume that if Ada married Willie, she would add precisely nothing to the quality of his life, and take nothing from it?

107/111   Ada
98/110   Love and marriage

110 WILLIE: That's what I've . . .
This interruption from Willie makes it quite plain that he will go with the winner of the battle. If Ada triumphs over Maggie, then Willie's loyalty to his promise will be honoured, but if Ada withdraws, then presumably Willie feels he is no longer under an obligation to her. He obviously has a strange, or perhaps well-developed, sense of what is and is not honourable.

Given what we know of the man and his background, do you find his attitude strange, or quite understandable? Can you justify your view by pointing to incidents and quotations from the play?

Willie states he doesn't love Maggie: does he love Ada? What do you think he understands the word to mean?

108/119	Willie
79/113	Choice and conflict
109/114	Love and marriage

111 ADA: You mind your . . .
A demonstration of a little spirit from Ada, but it will not amount to much, and she will live down to the description we have already been given of her character by the author.

109/116	Ada

112 MAGGIE: Not an atom. . . .
Is this really a fair contest? Maggie must surely know that Ada cannot compete with what she can offer Willie.

Be aware of the humorous nature of this scene, with Willie standing almost idly by as these two women argue about who is to have him.

107/161	Humour

113 ADA: I'm trusting him . . .
Ada's plans for Willie are as non-existent as Willie's plans for himself. Yet it is obvious that whilst Ada has no potential, Willie has. When Maggie put her conditions forward earlier, was it really a variation on Hobson's Choice? She knew there could be no competition from Ada, therefore there was only one logical outcome.

110/126	Choice and conflict

114 ADA [*weakly*]: It's daylight robbery. . . .
End of contest! One has to wonder at this point exactly how Ada and Willie managed to become engaged. Quite obviously, neither of them seemed to have had enough gumption to make the first move. However, all will shortly be revealed.

110/117	Love and marriage

115 MAGGIE: Will Mossop, you . . .
Maggie's ultimatum is typical of her determined and decisive approach to life and its problems.

Would you agree that Willie's response, 'Seems like there's no escape' is almost a sigh of relief? Could an actor say that line in a variety of different ways: frustrated, angry, helplessly, relieved? Try them, and see which you feel is most appropriate, and why.

The way in which the actor plays this line will be important in telling us something about Willie and his attitude to the events that have just happened.

104/118	Maggie
106/119	Play technique

116 ADA [*angry*]: Wait while I . . .
The shrewish nature of Ada is unleashed as she threatens Willie with her

111/0	Ada

mother. Note how Ada refers to her mother, almost as though she were a dog.

117 Maggie: Oh, so it's her . . .
The realization that Ada's mother was the matchmaker helps to explain how Willie and Ada came to be engaged. It also helps to explain why Willie is easily persuaded to swop Ada for Maggie.

118 Maggie: Well, can I . . .
Note the echo of how she dismissed Albert much earlier in this act. She offers Ada clogs, not expecting her to buy. She is merely using this as a means of propelling her out of the shop.

119 Willie [*rising*]: I'd really rather . . .
Would he really rather wed Ada? Or is Willie saying, 'I'd really rather not have a thick ear, Maggie'? His admission that he is afraid of Ada's mother gives us pause for thought. Should we see it as a black mark against his character, an indication of a weak-willed, easily frightened person? Or would this be played for its comic value, much as a large part of this scene would have been played? Certainly, it admits of this possibility, and the way that Willie shortly stands up to Hobson suggests that he is not really a coward.

120 Willie: It's like an 'appy . . .
It is obvious that Willie was never in love with Ada, merely driven into a corner by Ada's mother. Would you agree that having found himself in an impossible situation, he had simply decided to make the best of it? At least by marrying Ada he would have got her mother off his back, or would he? One can imagine that, like Hobson, Ada's mother saw him as just another source of income.

121 Willie: It's like an 'appy . . .
His comment that Maggie manages things is very apt.

122 Willie: And I don't agree . . .
Maggie may have won the day as far as Ada is concerned, and also gained her man, but he still has a mind of his own. Willie cannot bring himself to kiss Maggie quite so soon after the engagement, and especially not in front of her sisters, who mercifully arrive and give him an opportunity to escape.

So far as Willie is concerned, at this moment, enough is enough!

123 Maggie: He's a bit upset . . .
Do you find it strange that, almost in one breath, Maggie should first announce her engagement and then ask if dinner is ready? Are they of similar importance in her mind? Does her engagement mean very much to her? How would you explain her strange attitude? Did she add the bit about dinner merely to provoke her sisters?

Characters and ideas
previous/next comment

114/119 Love and marriage

115/121 Maggie

110/122 Willie
117/120 Love and marriage
115/136 Play technique

119/122 Love and marriage
104/140 Ambition and money

118/123 Maggie

119/132 Willie
120/123 Love and marriage

121/134 Maggie
122/124 Love and marriage

124 ALICE: You're going to marry . . .
Alice is outraged at Maggie's announcement. Why should having Willie as a brother-in-law affect her? Is Albert worth marrying if Maggie's choice of husband offends him? What does it say for his attitude to Alice, love and marriage, if her judgement of him is correct? In point of fact, is her judgement correct? Do we ever gain any evidence of his attitude in this matter?

35/179	Albert
38/145	Alice
123/145	Love and marriage

125 VICKEY: Father, have you heard . . .
Notice how Vickey is the first to leap in to acquaint Hobson with Maggie's news. Is she excited and happy for Maggie?

38/143	Vickey

126 HOBSON: News? There is . . .
The arrival of Hobson signals the moment the audience must now be waiting for. What will happen when Hobson hears the news? Who will win, Maggie or Hobson, and what will be the end result?

In one sense, the whole of this act has been an inexorable movement towards an inevitable conflict between two strong personalities, Maggie and her father. It will also lead to a crucial moment for Willie.

113/128	Choice and conflict
105/128	Structure

127 HOBSON: Marry – you – Mossop! . . .
The thought of Maggie's marrying, and of marrying Willie, are ideas that are totally incomprehensible to Hobson. He acts almost as though what had been said were totally irrelevant. Are his thoughts befuddled by drink so that he cannot appreciate the seriousness of what has just been said?

85/129	Hobson

128 [HOBSON *drives* ALICE *and* VICKEY . . .
He may drive his other two daughters out of the room, but Maggie is more used to doing the driving herself around here! The disappearance of Alice and Vickey leaves the stage clear for the battle between Hobson and Maggie.

126/130	Choice and conflict
126/141	Structure

129 HOBSON: I tell you . . .
Hobson's first argument concerns Willie's lowly origins. Maggie asks whether 'we're snobs in Salford'. The answer, as far as Hobson is concerned, is obviously yes. He is afraid of being laughed at. Yet again, it is selfish concerns that dominate his thoughts.

127/130	Hobson

130 MAGGIE: You will pay . . .
Maggie gives Hobson very reasonable terms as the conditions for her and Willie staying. However, his selfish and bullying nature refuses to consider her suggestion.

129/131	Hobson
128/132	Choice and conflict

131 MAGGIE: Cheap ones are . . .
This is quite a long speech for Maggie. The logic of it, however, is quite unacceptable to Hobson. Unable to deal with his daughter, he goes for what he considers to be the weak link, Willie. Do you remember the comment made to Mrs Hepworth about his being capable of making a man suffer? It is obviously his intention, now, to demonstrate how.

130/134	Hobson

132 MAGGIE: I'm watching you, . . .
This is Willie's first real test. He had been manoeuvred into his engagement with Ada, and had taken the easy way out. Perhaps he had done so with Maggie as well? However, now Hobson is bearing down on him, with every intention of taking out his drunken temper on him. Maggie's warning serves to sharpen our interest in what is about to happen. Might she break the engagement if Willie does not match up to her expectations?

122/133	Willie
130/133	Choice and conflict

133 WILLIE: I'm none wanting . . .
In the face of Hobson swinging the strap, Willie makes a spirited reply. In two short sentences he hits at the essence of the situation and demonstrates a determination that equals Maggie's. No doubt she listens with approval.

132/135	Willie
132/135	Choice and conflict

134 HOBSON: There's nobbut one answer . . .
Hobson gains his satisfaction by striking Willie, but it is a very short-lived satisfaction. That Hobson should have felt able to strike Willie with a belt says a lot about Victorian masters. Maggie is aghast that he has actually done such a thing. Does she learn something about her father here, and does it affect her attitude to him?

131/137	Hobson
123/141	Maggie

135 WILLIE: And I've nobbut . . .
Willie's response is everything that Maggie could have wished for. He acts with temper, yet with dignity. How well does his reaction fulfil the promise contained in the phrase 'raw material of a charming man'? Can you remember where this phrase occurred?

The threat he makes is just what Maggie wanted, but his action in kissing her is equally significant. He couldn't kiss her in front of her sisters, but here, five minutes later, he defiantly kisses her in front of her outraged father. This is a very different Willie from the 'rabbit' that jumped out of the trap in front of Mrs Hepworth.

133/136	Willie
133/137	Choice and conflict

136 MAGGIE: Willie! I knew . . .
Maggie is ecstatic. What is Willie's reaction: aghast at what he had done, amazed that he was able to do it, pleased, stunned? Either way, he seems quite unable to respond to Maggie's demonstration of joy.

If you were the actor, how would you play his reaction, and why?

135/159	Willie
119/137	Play technique

137 [HOBSON *stands in amazed indecision*]
Hobson is unable to make a choice. Events have turned out catastrophically wrong for him. In one fell swoop he has lost the daughter who made his shop a success, and the man who made his only saleable boots and shoes.

It is an appropriate moment to bring down the curtain on this act. Any more speeches or exits and entrances could only take away from the drama of the moment. All three characters on stage are struck in amazement at what has happened, and it has to be left to the audience's imagination if they want to know what happened immediately after. Wisely, the author does not attempt such a scene.

134/144	Hobson
135/139	Choice and conflict
136/138	Play technique

Commentary

Act Two

Act 2

138 *A month later. The shop . . .*
The scene description is important because it immediately suggests to the audience what happened as a result of the conflict between Maggie and Willie, and Hobson, in the final scene of the last act.

With Alice now in Maggie's chair we can sense that Maggie has left home. Vickey is reading; that hasn't changed.

137/195   Play technique

139 Alice: **I'm sure I . . .**
The helplessness of Alice, Vickey and Tubby is immediately evidenced. They are incapable of deciding what to do for the best. Orders for boots have dropped, as has the high class trade, and they are left with just clogs. Who suggested this would happen in the last act?

The bad temper and obvious frustration they demonstrate provide the setting for the appearance of a saviour, but more evidence of their helplessness is yet to come.

137/150   Choice and conflict

140 Tubby: **You know what's . . .**
The economic realities of the situation are voiced by Tubby. However, he is not in a position of authority, so he cannot make a decision. For another man this might have been a moment to grasp, to show his independence, skills and ambition, but not Tubby. Does he have any of these qualities?

52/142   Tubby
120/168   Ambition and money

141 Alice: **Oh, dear! What . . .**
The introduction of Maggie into the conversation, by Tubby, confirms to the audience that she has gone, and Alice's remark makes it clear that she is sorely missed, at least in so far as the shop is concerned. We are also rewarded with the information that the shop was more successful when she ran it. All in all, a satisfactory tribute to Maggie!

134/154   Maggie
128/144   Structure

142 Vickey: **You don't help . . .**
Tubby never did lay claim to being an intelligent foreman, but he is a match for Alice and Vickey. He is not about to start making decisions which could land him in trouble with Hobson.

140/168   Tubby

143 Vickey: **That's your look-out.**
Selfishness seems to be a Hobson trait. Vickey, a bit like Tubby, is not about to allow herself to be blamed for decisions that Alice makes.

125/146   Vickey

144 Vickey: **I don't blame you. . . .**
This piece of information gives the audience more of an insight into what has been happening since Maggie and Willie left. Apart from the poor business they are now doing, we learn that Hobson spends more time down at the 'Moonraker's' than ever before. It does not bode well for his business.

137/155   Hobson
141/148   Structure

145 Alice: **Well, it doesn't balance . . .**
For Alice, the problem of bookkeeping, which neither she nor Vickey seem up to, is easily solved by marriage. Is the suggestion that here she is responsible, but when married such matters will be her husband's concern?

124/160   Alice
124/147   Love and marriage

Does she not want responsibility? Does she see marriage as a cosy nest where she will be able to relax and leave everything to her husband?

146 ALICE: Well, you're sly, . . .
What did Hobson call Vickey? Can you remember his remark about gas meters? Is this reference to her being sly another insight into her character, or just a thoughtless comment from Alice?

143/156   Vickey

147 VICKEY: It's just as . . .
The reference to Maggie's spoiling their chances of marriage again raises the question of the meaning of love as far as their young men are concerned. Equally, it shows up Alice and Vickey in a poor light, in that they are prepared to marry just miserable specimens. Of course, we are assuming that their chances have been ruined and that Fred and Albert are indeed such specimens. Look for evidence on this matter as you read the rest of the play.

145/149   Love and
marriage

148 VICKEY: It's just as . . .
The reference to Maggie provides an appropriate cue for her to enter. Have you noticed how frequently such a cue is given in the play?

144/152   Structure

149 [MAGGIE *enters, followed by* . . .
Pay careful attention to this stage setting instruction, a great deal is mentioned. We could have guessed from the previous conversation that the 'carriage trade' was now served by Willie and Maggie, but we could not have known whether or not they were married.

0/151   Freddy
147/153   Love and
marriage
78/174   Setting

The introduction of Freddy Beenstock is interesting and important. His father's cellar will play a crucial part in the plot. Note how he is described. What do you imagine a 'blood' is? It is not a term we would use now. You will gain an idea if you ponder on what the description says he is, 'respectable son of a respectable tradesman'. Note how his 'appearance' is important to Vickey. Does it suggest for us what she views as being important in love?

150 VICKEY: I don't know . . .
The annoyance of Vickey and Alice is brought sharply into focus in this scene. What exactly are they criticizing Maggie for, and how justified do you think they are?

139/163   Choice and
conflict

151 FREDDY: It's very good . . .
How different is this, our first impression of Freddy, to that of Albert? How do you think their characters differ? This is but a short acquaintance, but we already know a fair bit about him.

149/176   Freddy

152 MAGGIE: . . . I see. He didn't . . .
The reference to the first scene when we met Albert assists in jogging our memories about what has gone before.

148/155   Structure

The need to get him from his office, and the reminder that he is a solicitor, or works in a solicitor's office, causes us to wonder what it is that Maggie is up to. The instruction 'to bring the paper with him' causes even more interest.

153 ALICE: Is it? Suppose . . .
They have learned nothing from Maggie's stand, and are still afraid of their father. Are they unable to leave because the men they want to marry can't afford to marry them, or are too weak to go against Hobson? Are the two girls also too weak to make a stand, both against Hobson and their two men, to gain the marriage they both so obviously desire?

149/161   Love and marriage

154 MAGGIE: I know. You . . .
Do you think Maggie is justified in her comment, and actually means it?

141/157   Maggie

155 FREDDY: You see, we've . . .
The description of Hobson sleeping his drunkenness off in a corn merchant's cellar indicates the extent to which he has fallen (no pun intended!) since we last met him.

144/203   Hobson
152/165   Structure

The suspense is being built up as we wonder what it is that Maggie has in mind, especially in view of Alice's and Freddy's comments about the difficulties that their marriage proposals have run into.

156 VICKEY: Fell? Is father hurt? . . .
Do you imagine that Vickey is really concerned about whether or not her father is hurt? You can only answer this question if you bear all the evidence in mind that we have at this moment. Equally, you need to consider exactly how Vickey speaks these words. Is she excited and pleased, or worried – and about what? Are her questions those of a worried, loving and dutiful daughter? How would you judge?

146/160   Vickey

157 MAGGIE: Don't. I've a job . . .
Maggie is no sooner back in the shop than she is organizing everyone. Does she change much during the course of the play?

154/158   Maggie

158 MAGGIE: The difference . . .
How much does Maggie's statement tell us about her character?

157/172   Maggie

159 WILLIE: It wasn't my fault, . . .
Willie's first remark since the last act. Has he changed at all, do you think, on the evidence of this remark? What else gives us an indication of how he views himself?

136/162   Willie

160 MAGGIE: Better, I say. . . .
No doubt Alice and Vickey are none too pleased to be described as mere shop assistants. How do you think they view themselves?

145/164   Alice
156/170   Vickey

161 WILLIE [*rising*]: Nay, Maggie, I'm . . .
This 'kissing' interlude is very amusing, as Maggie overcomes the reluctance of her sisters and Willie discovers that he quite likes kissing. However, there is more to it than that. Maggie is striving to gain acceptance for her husband,

112/179   Humour
153/162   Love and marriage

and is determined that her own sisters shall acknowledge him. He obviously has his customers' respect for the boots and shoes he makes, but Maggie wants the respect due to him as a man.

162 MAGGIE: You hold your hush. . . .
Willie's comment a little earlier, that he didn't know much about being the master in his own house or business, is given a little extra point here.

159/181   Willie
161/167   Love and marriage

163 MAGGIE: It's just a habit. . . .
That Maggie always gets her way is a tribute to her determination. It also highlights the fact that she would not get her own way if others had a more positive attitude towards their problems and were prepared to do a bit more than just moan about their lot.

Is the above a fair comment, and can you point to evidence in the text to support your view?

150/179   Choice and conflict

164 ALICE: I'll do it if . . .
For Alice, anything is preferable to doing her books. No more effective than Albert in a battle with Maggie, she fails to gain the latter's agreement to help her sort out the books. However, she kisses Willie.

160/166   Alice

165 WILLIE: There's more in kissing . . .
Maggie had been waiting for this moment for a while now. You will recall that in Act one she had wanted him to kiss her sisters, but he had bolted for his cellar.

155/175   Structure

166 MAGGIE: I've told you once. . . .
The attempt by Alice to command Maggie and perhaps pay her back for the boots Albert had to buy, fails miserably. However, she does at least try!

164/232   Alice

167 WILLIE: It's not a working . . .
The news that they are getting married today is dropped rather casually into the conversation by Willie. Are we to make any judgement as to the importance they attach to the event? If so, what, and why? Can we make any judgements on the matter? Do we have sufficient evidence?

162/169   Love and marriage

168 MAGGIE: Tubby can see to . . .
Tubby does have his uses! Maggie has obviously judged correctly as to the state of affairs at the shop. As a result, later when the offer of a partnership between Willie and Hobson is made, the ground has already been prepared.

142/182   Tubby
140/171   Ambition and money

169 ALICE: Wedded with a brass . . .
Quite obviously, Alice would not contemplate such a course. However, it is in keeping with Maggie's attitude as to what is and is not important. Can you remember her comments about courting, earlier in the play?

167/170   Love and marriage

170 VICKEY: I'll take good care . . .
Vickey's attitude to what is important is clear. No doubt she has a very clear view as to what Freddy Beenstock can provide her with. What other evidence do we have as to her attitudes?

160/172	Vickey
169/171	Love and marriage

171 ALICE: I'd stay single . . .
If it were left to Alice, she would stay single whether or not she could afford new furniture. Has Maggie any pride? How would you define pride, and perhaps more importantly, in what should we take pride? Can you define how the two daughters and their father differ in this matter from Maggie? Cite evidence from the text.

168/173	Ambition and money
170/172	Love and marriage

172 VICKEY: I'd start properly . . .
Vickey displays the same attitude as Alice, much to Maggie's satisfaction. Knowing that her sisters would never willingly give her and Willie anything, she has quite cleverly persuaded them to say they do not want, and would not want, second-hand furniture. She will now be free to take sundry items from the house, which is what she desired.

Would you agree that this was the only reason that Maggie and Willie came to the house? She says she has come to help them, yet is this the most important thing on her mind? She came for furniture: Willie has a hand-cart with him, as we shall see. She is going to get married that afternoon. She wants her sisters to be at the wedding, but how did she propose to help them to marry?

Was it just fortuitous that she met Freddy Beenstock, who presumably was hurrying to tell Alice and Vickey about their father's accident? Did Maggie just seize an opportunity? Would you agree the evidence suggests that she had not really come, initially, with any intention of helping her sisters?

158/178	Maggie
170/232	Vickey
171/173	Love and marriage

173 VICKEY and ALICE [together]: A cellar!
The two sisters obviously want to start life off in a different style to that of Willie and Maggie. The sparseness of their two cellars, the thrown-out furniture and the brass wedding ring all point to the poverty of Willie and Maggie. However, Maggie takes a long-term view of their lack of money, and is prepared to wait and work for it, much as she is prepared to wait for Willie to start loving her.

171/187	Ambition and money
172/181	Love and marriage

174 MAGGIE: Then it might as . . .
The reference to parlour and hand-cart help place the scene in its proper time.

149/177	Setting

175 VICKEY: Marriage portions, . . .
Having whet both their and the audience's appetite to know her plans, Maggie briskly turns to other matters. The reference a few lines down, to whether Albert had what Freddy asked for, increases the mystery slightly, but we shall not have to wait long for enlightenment. Note the hurried pace of this scene, where events quickly pile one on the other.

165/178	Structure

176 FREDDY: All right, Maggie.
Can you sense any difference between Freddy and Albert? Bear in mind not just the original stage direction as to his appearance and character, but also the easy relationship he appears to have with Maggie. He's obviously not used to being bossed around by a woman, yet how does he respond?

151/193   Freddy

177 MAGGIE: I thought it weren't . . .
It is perhaps appropriate to mention here the matter of Lancashire dialect. The author has not chosen to mystify the average reader or playgoer by making his characters speak in what would be to most a dense Lancashire accent. Rather, the northern setting is suggested by the occasional word and phrase which we do not normally meet, and which therefore gives the conversations a particular 'flavour'; such expressions as: 'you'll none rule me', 'owt', 'by gum', 'hold your hush', 'I'm none wanting', 'there's nobbut'. Look for others in the play. They are sprinkled fairly liberally throughout, but do not intrude upon the reader or listener.

174/184   Setting

178 ALBERT: It's what you told . . .
We now know what it is that Maggie has done, but the reason is not yet clear. Do her comments about lawyers remind you of another opinion on them earlier in the book?

172/181   Maggie
175/181   Structure

179 ALBERT: Yes, but to push . . .
Having dispatched Freddy to place the 'writ' for trespass and damages on her father's chest, Maggie now turns her attention to Albert. Do you think she enjoys getting the better of him and forcing him to do things against his will? Certainly, he could have refused to push the handcart through the streets, or perhaps put forward a good argument for doing it later when there might not be so many people around.

124/180   Albert
163/194   Choice and conflict
161/183   Humour

Albert's innate snobbishness comes very much to the fore here. Are he and Alice very similar in this respect, and can you think of other times when Alice demonstrates snobbishness?

180 ALBERT: . . . I suppose I must.
What is your opinion of Albert, and why? In answering such a question you must refer to incidents from the play which you feel demonstrate the character points you wish to make. Equally, you should use the occasional quotation – but do not forget to explain why you are using the quotation; they do not explain themselves.

179/193   Albert

181 WILLIE: I'm going through . . .
This short conversation between Willie and Maggie is important. It allows the author to satisfy the audience on the rightness of their marriage. Willie is shown as having begun to develop a mind and reasoning powers of his own, and Maggie is shown in a much more sympathetic light – she is not just a self-centred bully, determined to get her own way, as her father is.

178/187   Maggie
162/185   Willie
173/189   Love and marriage
178/188   Structure

182 MAGGIE: And time you were. . . .
Tubby is left in charge of the shop. Shortly he will have charge of everything.

168/242   Tubby

183 MAGGIE: I have. Do you . . .
There may be a greater understanding between Willie and Maggie, but she is not foolish enough to trust him with remembering the wedding ring.

179/192   Humour

Commentary

Act Three

Act 3

184 *The cellar in Oldfield Road . . .*
The detailed description of the cellars where Willie and Maggie are to live and work enables us to appreciate the starkness of their surroundings. It helps to emphasize their success in attracting the 'carriage trade' to their door, but also makes us understand why a year later they are ready to move out. It also acts as a contrast to the aspirations of Alice and Vickey. Do you imagine they would have been prepared to take it on as a place in which to both live and work?

177/239   Setting

185 *As the curtain rises, . . .*
Does the reference to Willie's reciting like a child who has learnt his lesson remind you of another reference to Willie and childhood? Is there a deliberate reference being made here which helps to suggest that he is changing, and emerging from his 'stunted' mental state?

181/186   Willie

186 WILLIE: **Oh, aye. That's it. . . .**
Is this the longest speech that Willie makes in the play? Even though he is being prompted by Maggie, and the speech was undoubtedly written by her, the mere fact that he actually gets up and faces his in-laws does suggest that he is changing, and for the better.

185/196   Willie

187 MAGGIE: **He'll do. Another . . .**
Maggie has faith in Willie, and is sure their future is probably more secure than those of Freddy and Albert. Do you think that financial security is the key element in Maggie's life?

181/190   Maggie
173/188   Ambition and money

188 ALBERT: **. . . Well, the start's . . .**
The question of where the capital comes from should remind us of the part played earlier by Mrs Hepworth.

65/236   Mrs Hepworth
187/189   Ambition and money
181/191   Structure

189 MAGGIE: **I? You mustn't call . . .**
This will not be the first time that Maggie pushes Willie forward. She obviously wants him to take his place amongst the men and with the appropriate status. Does it suggest to us that she does not see herself as 'ruling' her man, and does it also throw light on her attitudes towards both the business and marriage partnerships she has entered into?

188/207   Ambition and money
181/196   Love and marriage

190 MAGGIE: **Same place as those . . .**
Despite the probing questions, Maggie is not about to disclose the source of her finances. Proper business practice is obviously something that comes as second nature to Maggie.

187/199   Maggie

191 MAGGIE [*rising, as do the . . .*
The reference to their father brings him back to the audience's minds and reminds them of the writ that had been placed on his chest at the end of the

188/200   Structure

last act. Thus, when he makes an appearance later in this act, it will not seem an unexpected event.

192 FREDDY: But — you —
What is it that they find so amusing; the fact that the table is to be cleared, or that Willie is helping to clear up, or something else?

Does either Maggie or Willie give any evidence of being embarrassed by Albert and Freddy's amusement?

183/193	Humour

193 MAGGIE [*quite calmly*] . . .
It doesn't do to laugh at Willie. Maggie's immediate response is to require Albert and Freddy to do the washing up. Their, and Vickey's, outraged response shows that the smiles have been taken off their faces.

Notice how Maggie complains of Albert laughing. Didn't Freddy also laugh? Does this suggest that she has a deeper-rooted dislike of Albert than she has of Freddy? Would such an attitude be justified? Can you compare these two men and indicate with any degree of accuracy the differences between them? (Don't forget evidence and relevant quotations.)

180/198	Albert
176/198	Freddy
192/195	Humour

194 ALBERT [*after he and* FRED . . .
They have a fairly simple choice to make. Note the reasons they give for complying with Maggie's demand. Would they have done as they were told in any case, and merely justify the fact that they agree to do it?

179/201	Choice and conflict

195 WILLIE: I'm fond of a bit . . .
This humorous exchange could be played in a variety of ways. No doubt in many modern entertainments, a scene such as this would be played for its double-meaning potential and smut value. Here, the amusement of Albert and Freddy, and the innocent reluctance of Willie, is on a totally different level. The actors would have to be careful that they played their parts in accordance with the context of the play's atmosphere.

193/205	Humour
138/216	Play technique

196 WILLIE: That's a fact. . . .
There is no sense of embarrassment in the way Willie faces Albert and Freddy with his fears. Not for him the pretence that he is an experienced man and knows all about wedding nights that there is to know. Can the same be said of the other two men?

186/197	Willie
189/200	Love and marriage

197 WILLIE: It's that being alone . . .
Recall the phrase 'raw material of a charming man'? Do we see this aspect of Willie coming out here?

196/200	Willie

198 ALBERT: . . . That's not the way . . .
Are you critical of Albert and Freddy for their attitude here? Compared to Willie they are men about the world, but are they charming gentlemen? Or should we beware of judging them too severely on this matter?

193/223	Albert
193/0	Freddy

199 ALBERT: Aren't you at . . .
What does Maggie's answer to Albert's question say: that she is a domineering woman; that Albert and Freddy are weak characters and she knows it; or both?

200 [Knock at door upstairs, . . .
The knock on the door can really only be Hobson. Where were we partly prepared for such an event in this scene?

So far the wedding scene has largely concentrated on Willie's nervousness at what lies in front of him, a nervousness that prepares us for the comic moments to come. However, now we are to be brought back to a central issue, Hobson and his daughters' prospects.

201 MAGGIE: All right. We'll . . .
The consternation of the 'in-laws' at Hobson's arrival is laughable. For all Albert's and Freddy's worldliness, they are very weak vessels indeed when it comes to facing up to Hobson.

202 [The four go into . . .
The disappearance of the 'in-laws' clears the stage for the confrontation between Hobson, his daughter and Willie. Note Maggie's final instruction to Willie, 'you're gaffer here'. Has the status of Willie as her husband been mentioned before? It is a matter that will be referred to a few more times. Why does Maggie see it as being so important? Does Willie share her view at the moment, and will he change his attitude with time?

203 WILLIE: [loudly and boldly] . . .
This initial slight humiliation of Hobson helps to establish both the position of Willie as master, and also to ensure that Hobson is not in any commanding position. Do you think the latter is likely with Maggie around?

204 WILLIE: . . . Nay, but I am. . . .
We cannot but be reminded of the potential gentleman in Willie when we see the warmth of his greeting to his father-in-law. The last meeting we witnessed had the latter hitting Willie with a belt.

205 WILLIE: . . . Nay, but I am. . . .
Is part of Willie's enthusiastic greeting a matter of relief, that perhaps Hobson will stay a while and put off that much feared moment when he will be left alone with Maggie, as man and wife?

206 WILLIE: . . . A piece of pork pie . . .
Both Willie and Maggie ignore the obviously worried state that Hobson appears to be in. Both have different motives. Can you say what they are?

207 MAGGIE: Aye. But wedding cake's . . .
Do you find this remark from Maggie out of character? What rules her, head or heart? It would be easy to give a quick answer to this question, but what is required is a thoughtful answer. Think back to when Willie and Maggie had

Characters and ideas previous/*next* comment	
190/206	Maggie
197/203	Willie
196/202	Love and marriage
191/212	Structure
194/209	Choice and conflict
200/205	Love and marriage
155/208	Hobson
200/204	Willie
203/205	Willie
204/206	Willie
195/217	Humour
202/207	Love and marriage
199/207	Maggie
205/211	Willie
206/210	Maggie
189/208	Ambition and money

		Characters and ideas *previous*/*next* comment

a quiet word together just before they married: what ruled Maggie then? Is there any other evidence you should consider when making judgements about Maggie?

205/229	Love and marriage

208 HOBSON: Well, Maggie, you know . . .
What do you think of Hobson's response here? Is he being honest, or politic because he recognizes that he needs Maggie's advice? Again, the quick answer is not what is required here.

203/209	Hobson
207/215	Ambition and money

209 MAGGIE [*holding plate*] . . .
Maggie's comment, on the surface, is to the effect that she expects her father to eat the wedding cake, whether he likes it or not. However, is there another, underlying meaning here? Is she suggesting that Hobson has only himself to blame for the situation he is in, and must suffer the consequences? Not quite 'you've made your bed and now you must lie on it', but close enough?

208/213	Hobson
201/242	Choice and conflict

210 MAGGIE [*rising and going* . . .
Does Maggie really mean to leave Willie and Hobson to discuss the matter, or is this just yet another determined effort to make Willie accept and live up to the responsibilities that his position now demands?

207/219	Maggie

211 MAGGIE: Private from Will? . . .
Willie's position is important to Maggie. Not only does she want him to achieve his real potential, but equally she wants to feel that she has married a man, not a doormat.

Note how Willie tells Hobson to sit down – he is beginning to 'find his feet'. But the effect is somewhat spoiled when he is astonished that he should call Hobson 'father'. However, the audience can begin to see that Willie is altering – certainly he is no longer the 'rabbit' who cowered when Mrs Hepworth told him to 'Take that'.

You ought to be able to trace and relate the various stages by which Willie changes and gradually gains in stature.

206/212	Willie

212 HOBSON: That – [*producing* . . .
For the second time, Willie is given something he cannot read, but to be fair to him this is rather more substantial than a visiting card. Equally, it also serves as a visual reminder that he is growing in status, even though he holds it upside down.

211/216	Willie
200/214	Structure

213 HOBSON: Maggie, I say it . . .
Note the long speeches of Hobson. He has not changed in this respect. He takes a very long time to say nothing at all that is of use to Maggie.

209/214	Hobson

214 HOBSON: It's an accident. . . .
The fear of lawyers that he expressed at an earlier stage has echoes of Maggie's own caustic comments on the subject recently: can you remember when and in what circumstances?

213/218	Hobson
212/221	Structure

215 HOBSON: Wonder! [*He rises and . . .*
Note Hobson's major concerns, loss of money and loss of status in the community. If he were realistic about the matter, would he agree that he no longer has much of either to lose?

208/220   Ambition and
money

216 WILLIE: Eh, by gum, think . . .
Willie's innocent enjoyment at the thought of appearing in a newspaper contrasts with Hobson, aghast at the prospect.

212/217   Willie
195/235   Play technique

Note the stage direction about there being no malice in his comment regarding the satisfaction such a report might give to others. The author's intention is clearly stated, and leaves the actor no room at all to play this with even a hint of enjoyment at Hobson's discomfort. What would have been the effect of such an interpretation on our assessment of Willie's character?

217 WILLIE [*sincerely*]: Nay, it's not. . . .
No malice is needed on Willie's part. With this very humorous and sincere comment, Willie twists the knife in the wound yet again.

216/228   Willie
205/226   Humour

Hobson's wry comment provokes a spirited response from Willie.

218 HOBSON: I didn't come to . . .
Hobson's angry outburst is quickly stilled by Maggie. It is quite obvious that he really doesn't want any advice from Willie.

214/227   Hobson

219 MAGGIE: It's the publicity . . .
Is it the publicity that Hobson is most afraid of? Certainly Maggie wants him to think so, as she shortly comes back to the fact that the matter may be settled in private. Why is she so determined to persuade Hobson of the benefits of avoiding publicity?

210/233   Maggie

220 HOBSON [*coming back to . . .*
Having carefully laid the ground, Maggie now produces her 'rabbit' from the hat, much to Hobson's amazement. What is he more concerned with, the publicity or the money?

215/224   Ambition and
money

221 HOBSON [*with disgust almost . . .*
The abhorrence that Hobson feels for lawyers is perhaps the key to his eventually agreeing to the terms he will be presented with. The author has prepared the ground thoroughly, and the audience should not find the logic of the following developments at all strange. Can you trace the various stages by which we have been prepared for this event? Don't overlook Albert's occupation!

214/222   Structure

222 HOBSON [*shaking his head, . . .*
The question as to who is looking after the shop allows the conversation to move quite naturally on to Alice and Vickey, their duties in the shop and Hobson's attitude to their getting married. And thus nicely back to the matter of Maggie's plan, and the reason that Hobson has turned up on her doorstep.

221/236   Structure

223 ALBERT: Hadn't we better . . .
Do you notice the change in Albert? A few moments ago he was hiding in Maggie's bedroom, suffering the same worries as the others as to what Hobson might or might not do and say. Now he is taking charge of the situation.

198/0	Albert

224 HOBSON [*turning on him* . . .
Do you think that perhaps, given the greed of Albert that is about to be demonstrated, Hobson has a valid point in what he says about lawyers?

220/225	Ambition and money

225 ALBERT: The sum we propose, . . .
Albert's figure is greeted with astonishment by Hobson, and instant rejection by Maggie. Her comment about Albert's greed amply supports Hobson's view of the nature of lawyers. Note how Albert and Freddy had obviously agreed this figure in advance.

224/226	Ambition and money

226 HOBSON [*rising*]: Maggie, you've saved me . . .
She hasn't saved him, but by a quirk of fortune it does appear to him that she has reduced his costs. However, she is not so foolish as to encourage him into thinking much further on the lines of a counter-claim. Note his own foolish pride when he refuses to be thought of as a pauper, and admits that he could afford the five hundred pounds that she wants him to pay.

Note how Vickey makes use of that pride when she reminds him that he isn't beaten when, having been asked for a thousand pounds, he only gives five hundred.

225/234	Ambition and money
217/231	Humour

227 HOBSON [*picking up his hat*] . . .
Typical of Hobson's bluster, he now vents his anger on all and sundry. Is his threat to staff his shop with men as empty as the rest of his speeches have been? Can you remember any time when he did not bluster, but acted?

218/228	Hobson

228 HOBSON: Will Mossop, I'm sorry . . .
Can you understand what drives Hobson to be 'nice' to Willie? Is he being nice to him?

227/230	Hobson
217/234	Willie

229 HOBSON: I kept you, didn't I? . . .
There is a rather ironic reference here in his talk of their marriage responsibilities. It is those very matters which two of his daughters will use as an excuse not to look after him.

207/230	Love and marriage

230 HOBSON [*turning*]: Aye. You . . .
Do you think his last utterance on the subject of marriage gives us an insight as to his own experiences? Can you list the attitudes he has expressed on various occasions about the subject, and summarize how he views matrimony?

228/241	Hobson
229/231	Love and marriage

231 WILLIE: No. No. [*He rises*] . . .
Throughout the excitement of Hobson's downfall, what has been occupying Willie's mind? Maggie is not going to countenance any further disturbance of her plans for the evening, and Willie has to give way.

226/237	Humour
230/232	Love and marriage

232 VICKEY [*with a quick kiss*] . . .
How should you judge the kisses that both Alice and Vickey give Maggie? Is there an element of true sisterly love here, or is it just a thoughtless and momentary reward for Maggie's assistance? Who, or what, do these two love the most?

166/268	Alice
172/270	Vickey
231/237	Love and marriage

233 MAGGIE: And you've got me. . . .
Would you agree that this is a moment of real affection on Maggie's part? Affection tempered by a clear appreciation of the realities of the situation they are in?

219/234	Maggie

234 MAGGIE [*sitting at the table* . . .
Do we gather that the sentence Willie wrote was not of Maggie's direction? If so, do we have the first real indication of the ambitions that are stirring in Willie's mind?

The sentence she writes is equally pointed at the future and leaves us in no doubt as to her attitude.

233/259	Maggie
228/275	Willie
226/241	Ambition and money

235 [WILLIE *takes her place* . . .
Notice the small but very atmospheric actions of Maggie. What do these stage instructions say to us about her and Willie?

216/247	Play technique

236 I'll put these flowers . . .
The secret of where Willie and Maggie gained their capital in order to start up in marriage and business is revealed. Not an important remark on her part, but an indication of how careful the author has been in his structuring of the play to tie up any loose ends, should the audience not have guessed for themselves.

188/0	Mrs Hepworth
222/238	Structure

237 [*Exit* MAGGIE *to the bedroom,* . . .
The final scene is full of amusement: Willie's indecision, his settling down on an uncomfortable sofa, and finally facing the door – his fate; whence Maggie soon emerges to lead him to bed by the ear. Is there any sense in which the audience is encouraged to laugh at Willie in this scene?

231/246	Humour
232/252	Love and marriage

238 [*Exit* MAGGIE *to the bedroom,* . . .
Maggie and Willie have settled into their own bedroom. Alice and Vickey have departed with their fiancés, secure in the knowledge that they will be able to marry. Hobson has scurried off, shouting, to absolutely no consequence at all – all his plans frustrated by Maggie. Mrs Hepworth's part in all this has been disclosed; Tubby and Jim Heeler played too small a part to warrant any more notice being taken of them. Should the play have ended here?

236/240	Structure

Commentary

Act Four

Act 4

	Characters and ideas previous/next comment	

239 *The scene represents . . .*
Read the scene description carefully. Do you think it represents the values that Hobson holds, or held, dear? The re-introduction of Tubby, incompetently cooking bacon and trying to lay the table, indicates the extent to which Hobson has sunk. Are we to take it that Tubby no longer has any work to do in the shop?

184/244 Setting

240 TUBBY: **I told you what . . .**
The information that Tubby has been for the doctor, that Hobson is ill, but that he is getting up for breakfast, poses some questions for the audience. Is Hobson really ill, or just full of self-pity? What does he need Jim Heeler for?

238/246 Structure

At the end of the last act it seemed as though all the loose ends had been tied up, but here, suddenly, we have a new development, albeit a year later. No doubt the audience wonders what has happened in that year, not only to Hobson, Vickey and Alice, but more particularly to Maggie and Willie.

241 TUBBY [*cutting the bread*]: **Every way . . .**
The depths to which Hobson and his business have descended are amply witnessed by Tubby here, and further down the page.

230/242 Hobson
234/245 Ambition and money

242 TUBBY: **Don't you? I'm an . . .**
What do you think of Tubby here? Does he demonstrate an unexpected loyalty to Hobson, and is that loyalty justified by the treatment he has received? A relatively minor part, Tubby takes on an unexpected depth of character. Does he really have any choice in what he does? Given his probable age and lack of real skills, what would be his alternative if he now left his employer? How would he survive? Or do such considerations occur to him? What do you think?

241/243 Hobson
182/243 Tubby
209/251 Choice and conflict

What do you think of his assessment as to what is ruining the shop? Can you think of any evidence concerning the character of Hobson that would support Tubby's opinion?

243 TUBBY: **Willie's a good lad, . . .**
Do you think Willie or Maggie would agree that Willie learnt his trade and skills from Tubby? Will we ever know the truth or otherwise of that statement? If Tubby trained Willie, why can't Hobson's shop produce the goods that would attract the 'carriage trade' back to them? Is it really only a lack of tact on Hobson's part?

242/245 Hobson
242/244 Tubby

244 JIM: **Cost more than women.**
It would appear that, true to his threat, Hobson employs men assistants in his shop. Despite Jim's suggestion that women might find men assistants appealing, Tubby has the last, and probably correct word on the subject. 'Ladies' weren't just females.

243/0 Tubby
239/249 Setting

245 HOBSON [*with acute melancholy . . .*
All the bluster and bounce would appear to have been knocked out of

243/246 Hobson

Hobson. How would you describe the difference between him now, and in earlier scenes? Was he self-centred and self-pitying then?

Would you say he has lost his will to fight and the ambition to acquire money?

246 TUBBY [*getting the bacon*] . . .
The humorous potential of this scene would need to be exploited – can you see what it is?

Tubby's constant reference to getting Maggie, and Hobson's lack of interest in the subject, is enough to ensure that the audience can guess Tubby will go for her. How are we to take Hobson's remark that he is a dying man?

247 HOBSON: I'm dirty now. . . .
Again, we have to ask how we are to take a remark. The author will have had a clear picture in his mind as he wrote these lines, as to the manner in which they should be played. Yet, how are they to be played? We shall shortly hear that Hobson is indeed dying, if he doesn't stop drinking. So his words about washing and his razor could be played quite 'straight'. Yet on the other hand we have the author's instructions that he is full of self-pity and melancholy, which does rather prejudice us against him. Is the audience supposed to find his state amusing?

You might like to attempt the various registers in which his speeches could be interpreted. Note there is not necessarily any conflict between his illness and the author's attitude towards him.

248 HOBSON: 'Moonraker's.'
Hobson's admission of the cause of his troubles speaks of some reality in his mind. It also sets the scene nicely for the Doctor's view of his illness.

249 JIM [*speaking without indicating* . . .
You may wonder at the author's stage direction, 'He does not rise'. In Victorian times, a grocer most certainly should have deferred to a doctor. At the very least, good manners would have dictated that he rose when company entered – it happens even today.

250 DOCTOR: Hum. Not much to . . .
Jim's ill-mannered conduct, and the fact that the Doctor has been up all night, perhaps explain the shortness of his temper. Certainly the Doctor is quick to judge what ails Hobson, and what will ail Jim.

251 DOCTOR: If ye want flattery, . . .
The final rout of Hobson is about to take place. Beginning with the Doctor, we shall see how he manages to fare. The audience will sense that a clash of wills is about to take place, a clash that will leave Hobson with some difficult choices to make.

Characters and ideas previous/next comment	
241/254	Ambition and money
245/248	Hobson
237/247	Humour
240/258	Structure
246/261	Humour
235/255	Play technique
246/251	Hobson
76/0	Jim Heeler
244/276	Setting
0/253	Dr MacFarlane
248/252	Hobson
242/253	Choice and conflict

252 DOCTOR: Your complaint and . . .
What do you imagine led Hobson down to the 'Moonraker's' in the first place, and what kept him there? Is this a clue to the Doctor's remark about his character and complaint? What do you understand it to mean?

251/253   Hobson
237/264   Love and
           marriage

253 DOCTOR: Sir, if I am . . .
Annoyed by Jim's comment, and his continued presence, which Hobson has done nothing about, the Doctor decides to go, and is decidedly direct in his remark to Jim.

The fact that Hobson decides to tell Jim to go, rather than the Doctor, suggests that perhaps he really does need his services and that he is not prepared to wait for another. Is his remark about teaching the Doctor a lesson mere bravado?

250/257   Dr MacFarlane
252/256   Hobson
251/258   Choice and
           conflict

254 HOBSON: If you calculate . . .
Perhaps Hobson views doctors in the same light as lawyers, and is suspicious of what they'll do to his bank balance. Certainly he has delayed calling one in for perhaps too long a time for his own good.

245/274   Ambition and
           money

255 DOCTOR: And do you seriously . . .
Hobson's condition is obviously serious. He has already recognized the cause himself, so why has he asked the Doctor in? Is the answer in his self-pity? Does he require others to know of his condition so that he may more publicly enjoy the pity that he feels for himself?

The way in which the actor plays this sequence will be crucial in determining how the audience reacts to his illness.

247/275   Play technique

256 HOBSON: Much use your . . .
It seems a bit foolish to pay for advice and then not take it. However, the character of Hobson has also to be taken into account. The degree of self-pity he feels overcomes the Doctor's good sense. Perhaps Hobson is beginning to feel as though he is a martyr in some obscure cause – revenge on his daughters?

253/263   Hobson

257 DOCTOR [*putting his hat down,* . . .
The realization that Hobson really is determined to go down to the 'Moonraker's' for another drinking session gives the Doctor pause for thought. He is not going to walk away from his patient when there is a hope of saving him.

To what extent is the Doctor a figure against which we can contrast Hobson? Of a similar age to him, and described in the stage directions as 'domineering', he is a fighter. Is Hobson?

253/258   Dr MacFarlane

258 DOCTOR: . . . Do ye ken that . . .
The doctor is not prepared to give his patient any choice in the matter of living and dying. In so doing, he forewarns us of the final choice that Hobson will have to make.

257/261   Dr MacFarlane
253/260   Choice and
           conflict
246/259   Structure

259 DOCTOR: Maggie? Then I'll tell . . .
The reintroduction of Maggie as the possible saviour for Hobson's life brings us full circle. At the beginning of the play, it was she who ensured that the shop was profitable and supported Hobson in his life of drinking – albeit neither willingly nor intentionally. Now she is being brought back to ensure that he stays alive, without drinking.

234/266	Maggie
258/262	Structure

260 DOCTOR: You'll have to have . . .
Again, a reference to Hobson having no choice in a matter. This theme is gathering greater and greater importance as we near the end of the play.

What is it about the characters of the Doctor and Hobson that should lead the former to take a liking to the latter?

258/265	Choice and conflict

261 DOCTOR: If she's the woman . . .
A quite accurate and amusing summing up from the Doctor as to the likely qualities that Maggie will bring to her father's sick-bed.

258/0	Dr MacFarlane
247/0	Humour

262 MAGGIE: What about me?
Do you find some of these entrances that are so exactly on cue perhaps a little too obvious? Certainly they are exactly right in terms of the smooth movement and development of the plot, but do they ever jar? Not an easy question, and one which requires a great deal of sensitive response to the artistic crafting of the play. You should not expect to give a simple yes or no answer, and there simply is not a right answer. But do think on the matter, when you have time!

259/272	Structure

263 MAGGIE: I've come because . . .
The news that Tubby fetched Maggie does not go down well. But Hobson shouldn't really complain; he did after all tell Tubby that he didn't care what he did in this respect. Are we to make any judgements on Hobson for his 'sacking' of Tubby?

256/267	Hobson

264 HOBSON: Just nasty-minded curiosity.
Of Hobson's three daughters, could this remark be fairly addressed to any one of them? If you feel it could, then you should have evidence in the form of reference to incidents, and quotation, to back up your judgement.

252/269	Love and marriage

265 HOBSON: That's right, Maggie. . . .
Unable to 'teach the doctor a lesson' himself, Hobson is reduced to cheering Maggie on. Yet he totally misreads the situation. Maggie is not 'seeing the doctor off', merely establishing her own position and responsibilities in the matter.

260/271	Choice and conflict

266 HOBSON: You ask Will Mossop! . . .
The speed with which Maggie tells Tubby to get Willie obviously indicates that she sees an opportunity here.

Hobson's remark that sending for Willie is an excuse needs to be examined. If it is an excuse, then Maggie is not succeeding in her desire to develop Willie's potential; equally, all her actions in this respect are a sham. Would such a situation be in keeping with the Maggie we have come to know?

259/267	Maggie

Would you agree that there is an element of truth in Hobson's remarks, and if so, how would you defend that view, using evidence from the text and not just unsubstantiated opinions?

267 MAGGIE: My husband's my husband, . . .
Annoyed at Hobson's constant remarks about her husband, Maggie loses patience. However, as will be noted a few lines further on, Hobson doesn't learn very easily. Note how he dismisses Willie with the phrase, 'I'll give him claims'. If he wants to influence Maggie in his favour, he is going the wrong way about it.

263/283	Hobson
266/279	Maggie

268 [ALICE enters L. She is rather . . .
We are given a clear indication of Alice's new status and view of life in this short description of her.

Her cutting remark about the wife of a cobbler, the reference to Maggie having to get up early, and to her own elevated position as a solicitor's wife, leave us in no doubt as to the nature of her character. It all serves to confirm that the kiss she gave Maggie on the wedding night meant absolutely nothing to her.

The comment she makes to Hobson shows she is not really interested in his welfare. One wonders why she came in response to Tubby's call; perhaps just out of curiosity?

232/269	Alice

269 HOBSON: And I say you're—
The coldness of Alice and the lack of concern she coolly demonstrates at last seem to penetrate Hobson. As the text says, we don't learn what he wanted to say, but it doesn't take much sense to imagine it.

268/280	Alice
264/270	Love and marriage

270 VICKEY: Father, you're ill! . . .
The artificiality of Vickey's greeting hardly needs commenting on. She is as much concerned about her father's health as she was about his business, when she spent all her time reading in the shop. The excuse that she is expecting a baby makes her determination not to return home quite plain for all to see.

232/273	Vickey
269/272	Love and marriage

271 HOBSON [rising]: Of course I . . .
The conniving, sarcastic and derogatory remarks that Alice, Vickey and Hobson make about Willie are not very wise, given the circumstances. Hobson is going to pay dearly for them, and both Vickey and Alice will have cause to be angry.

265/277	Choice and conflict

272 MAGGIE: I see. You've got . . .
How accurately does Maggie sum up the attitudes of her two sisters?

At the end of the last act we remarked that it seemed the play had drawn to an effective conclusion. However, it is now obvious that it was a 'false conclusion'. We were left with an inaccurate picture of Alice and Vickey making friends with their sister, but in reality it seems very likely that since that day, they have not come near her. We have to make a different assessment of their characters, and especially so in the light of the attitudes they demonstrate towards their father.

270/274	Love and marriage
262/278	Structure

Equally, it seemed at the end of Act three that Hobson had been overcome – not so. He is still a self-centred, opinionated bully. And perhaps worst of all, like his other two daughters, he has no respect for Willie.

There would appear to be very good reasons why the play needs a final act.

---

273 VICKEY: Oh, do stop talking . . .

The comment that Willie 'hasn't the spirit of a louse' is a pretty nasty remark. Is there evidence earlier in the play of Vickey's spiteful tongue?

270/280	Vickey

---

274 VICKEY: Can't you see what . . .

The two loving daughters really have only one thing on their minds, Vickey particularly so.

254/275	Ambition and money
272/289	Love and marriage

---

275 ALICE: That's never Willie Mossop.

Alice's remark is important. Ever since Maggie came into this act, there have been constant attacks on Willie, and she has been attempting to defend him. The audience has been left in a state of uncertainty as to what the truth actually is. Alice's remark, followed by the stage directions, shows the true picture. He has changed, and is a very different man from the one we met at the start of the play.

Do remember that stage directions are not something that the audience 'see' in front of them as the reader does. It is assumed throughout this commentary, and by the author when he puts in the stage directions, that the audience will be aware of those directions through the expertise of the play's director and the actors.

234/276	Willie
274/278	Ambition and money
255/0	Play technique

---

276 WILLIE: Now, then, Maggie, . . .

The difference in Willie is immediately obvious. The commands he gives to Maggie are to the point. He is a busy man and cannot waste time. However, she still has a contribution to make to his education – note how she takes his hat off him. It was polite, and still is, for a man to take his hat off when he enters a house. It is not a matter of great moment in modern times, as so few men now wear hats.

275/277	Willie
249/0	Setting

---

277 WILLIE: If you'd not married . . .

Vickey's opinion about Willie's spirit (what was it?) is shown to be very wide of the mark, as he proceeds to do more than hold his own with them.

His remark a few lines on about how times have changed, and his comments about the help he and Maggie gave them in getting a start in married life, firmly establish for Alice, Vickey and the audience that Willie has indeed changed. It helps to create an air of suspense as well. He will shortly meet Hobson, and the audience is looking forward to a conflict on more even terms than before.

276/278	Willie
271/281	Choice and conflict

---

278 WILLIE: Good morning, father. . . .

A neat little structural link with the previous act. Do you remember how Willie had to be told by Maggie that he could address Hobson as 'father'. He needs no reminding now.

Willie's comment about the state of Hobson's business does not go down

277/279	Willie
275/281	Ambition and money
272/280	Structure

very well, and he makes it quite clear that his business is rather more important to him than Hobson's life. This is most certainly a changed Willie Mossop.

279 WILLIE: What's to do? . . .

Quite obviously, Willie and Maggie have discussed how this matter should be approached, and Willie has had his instructions. Does this suggest that Maggie determines things in their household, or is there more to the matter than that?

267/288	Maggie
278/286	Willie

280 HOBSON: That doesn't come . . .

This spirited attack from Hobson takes his two daughters by surprise. He has seen through them and their excuses, and at last has the sense to show them the door. However, whilst he has read their characters correctly, he has made a great mistake over Willie.

The exit of Alice and Vickey signals the end of their part in the play. Their characters have been well explored, and the audience has had the satisfaction of knowing that they have been found out for what they really are. So far as they are concerned, the author really has tied all the loose ends up.

269/0	Alice
273/0	Vickey

281 WILLIE: It may be news . . .

This is no offer that Willie finds himself unable to reject. The proposition has absolutely no attraction for Willie or Maggie, and if accepted would merely put them back a year to where they were before all these events had happened. It did nothing at all to match up with their ambitions.

278/282	Ambition and money
277/284	Choice and conflict

282 WILLIE: All right, I will. . . .

This is very much a new man speaking. He is articulate and forceful. His analysis of the relative merits of their businesses is closely argued and compulsive. We saw earlier in this act sure signs that Hobson's business was failing, now we get chapter and verse on the matter. Willie and Maggie have made good their intentions of over a year ago to form a partnership that would succeed.

281/286	Ambition and money

283 HOBSON: But–but–you're Will . . .

Hobson finds it difficult to come to terms with Willie's statement. Not because he can dispute the facts of what he says, but simply because it is Willie saying it. As yet he cannot come to terms with the change that has occurred in Willie.

267/0	Hobson

284 WILLIE: I'm doing well, . . .

The proposition that Willie puts is very fair, fairer perhaps than Hobson could have expected, given his past attitude. Is this the 'Hobson's Choice' of the title? Take it or leave it? Does Hobson really have any option at all in the matter, if he is not to drink himself to death in the next few months?

281/285	Choice and conflict

285 HOBSON: I'm not dead, yet, . . .

Not a very strong rejoinder from Hobson. The partnership arrangements have been accepted without any effective objection, and the only dispute relates to whether or not Hobson is 'late'. Well, that isn't actually in

284/287	Choice and conflict

question, but effectively, as both a father and a businessman, he is a spent force. His protests are inconsequential and ignored by both Willie and Maggie.

*Characters and ideas
previous/next comment*

286 WILLIE: It's no farther . . .
The authority with which Willie moves about the shop deciding how it will change speaks of a man who knows his own mind. The comments he makes about the likelihood of eventually moving to a shop in Saint Ann's Square demonstrate the strength of his ambition, and the audience can have little doubt in their minds that he will achieve it.

279/288 Willie
282/0 Ambition and money

287 HOBSON [*looking pathetically* . . .
Along with a meek 'Yes, Maggie' at the end of the play, these are Hobson's final words. He has been most things in this play, but never pathetic. The loose end has been properly tied, and the audience have the satisfaction of seeing all his bullying and bluster finally overcome. The end of Act three was not completely satisfactory because it left him and his threats as a potential danger to the smooth course of Willie and Maggie's future. The same cannot be said now, as they move off to the solicitor's office to settle the matter legally.

285/0 Choice and conflict
280/0 Structure

288 WILLIE: Did I? Yes . . .
But a small element of self-doubt on Willie's part. Not a weakness, but a sign of the charming man that was promised when we first met him.

279/0 Maggie
286/0 Willie

Note the small part Maggie has played in this scene. Apart from protesting about the 'late Hobson', she has taken little part in the discussions. Quite obviously they had discussed the matter beforehand, but this was no inept wedding speech, half memorized for the day of their wedding partnership. This was the confident speech of a man intent on forging a business partnership that was of advantage to him. Willie has moved on in the world, in every sense.

289 MAGGIE: Don't spoil it, . . .
Is there any sense here of the feeling that having 'made' him, Maggie feels she 'owns' him?

274/290 Love and marriage

290 MAGGIE: You'll not do owt . . .
This is a partnership in which Maggie is determined to have her say. But the key word is partnership, and it is difficult to imagine either of them trying to take advantage of, or bullying the other.

289/291 Love and marriage

291 MAGGIE: I'm not preventing you. . . .
The small dispute over the matter of the ring shows that Maggie still has her feet firmly on the ground.

290/0 Love and marriage

Their love for each other finds a totally adequate expression in their words 'Eh, lad!' and 'Eh, lass!'. The audience can appreciate the depth of the relationship that has been forged, and depart in the satisfaction of knowing the play has reached its correct conclusion.

Characters in the play

This is a very brief overview of each character. You should use it as a starting point for your own studies of characterization. For each of the aspects of character mentioned, you should look in your text for evidence to support or contradict the views expressed here, and indeed, your own views as well.

Know the incidents and conversations which will support and enlarge upon your knowledge of each character. You will find it helpful to select a character and follow the commentary, referring always to the text to read and digest the context of the comment.

Hobson

From the start, Hobson is a blustering, self-centred bully. He thinks very little of his daughters and workmen, and only considers as important what he does for them (which is little enough) and never what he gets from them.

The expertise of Maggie as a saleslady, and of Willie as a craftsman, are what keeps Hobson in money and leisure, allowing him to spend too much time at the 'Moonraker's', drinking.

As you read the play, you must be aware of the gradual decline in Hobson's fortunes, and be able to trace the various stages in that decline. Note also how his relationships with his daughters change, particularly so with Maggie. Be aware of how he continually underestimates the capacity of others to improve themselves and change their lives.

Maggie

The eldest daughter, Maggie is the driving force behind the success of Hobson's shop. However, her father has no appreciation of her personal desires and aspirations, and is calculatedly damning of her marriage prospects. (He knows very well that she is the key to his fortunes, and cannot afford to lose her.)

Frustrated by her life, Maggie sees in Willie the chance to escape from spinsterhood and drudgery in her father's shop and house. Note that however much she might ride roughshod over the likes of Albert and her sisters, when it comes to Willie and her own future, she adopts a more sensitive approach. She may drive Willie into an engagement, but she is not prepared to force him into an unwilling marriage. Her and her sisters' attitudes to love and marriage are a central theme of the play.

Does Maggie change during the course of the play, or do we just get to know her better?

Willie

A central character: the changes we witness in Willie during the course of the play act as a background against which we can chart all the other events. He starts off unappreciated, downtrodden and ignorant. By the end, he has become that 'charming man' which the author's character sketch prophesied.

At times amusing, at others bewildered and unsure of himself, Willie is often the occasion of laughter; but whilst other characters may laugh at Willie, this is rarely, if ever, the audience's reaction. Can you say why this is?

His relationship with Maggie leads to his developing his full potential, and you must be aware of the detailed course of that development.

Alice and Vickey

These two provide clear pictures of greed, insensitivity, self-centredness and ingratitude. They are snobbish, and their views of love and marriage are in stark contrast to Maggie's.

Their attempts to leave home and marry, and the worries they have about their men-friends' reactions to Maggie's marrying Willie, ensure the audience has no sympathy for them at all. They do manage, with Maggie's help, to get married, but one can only doubt whether those marriages will be very happy.

Albert and Freddy

The two men that Alice and Vickey marry have a relatively small part to play. As a solicitor, Albert is useful for drawing up the writ against Hobson, and fortuitously, it was the cellar of Freddy's father that Hobson fell into, thus enabling the writ to be issued.

They are also useful in acting as contrasts to Willie and his attempts to better himself. Neither of these two men has much in his favour, but you ought to consider whether the author presents Freddy in a slightly better light than Albert.

Mrs Hepworth and Dr MacFarlane

Mrs Hepworth makes a very minor appearance. Her main function is to assist the structuring of the play, by commenting on and thus 'proving' Willie's skill as a shoemaker. Secondly, she provides the enabling mechanism whereby the author can justify Willie and Maggie's being able to set up in business.

Dr MacFarlane provides a nice contrast to Hobson, perhaps as an indication of what Hobson might have amounted to if he drank a bit less, and was less self-centred. He makes but one appearance, and in doing so sets the scene for Hobson's final downfall.

Ada, Tubby and Jim Heeler

Ada was, for a short while, Willie's fiancée. A spineless creature, she was ruled by her mother and would have been totally unsuitable as a wife for Willie. She enables the audience to judge just how much Maggie was able to do for Willie, if they dwell for a moment on what his fate might have been had he married Ada.

Tubby is the faithful retainer; or is he? Does he stay at Hobson's because he has neither the will nor the ability to better himself? Is he a prime example of what Willie might have become if Maggie hadn't rescued him?

Jim Heeler, Hobson's drinking companion, really has one major function in the play: to enable Hobson to open his mind to the audience. He is a slight figure and plays a fairly inconsequential part in the action.

What happens in each act

Act 1

A very full act, with all the major characters sketched in, together with the main themes of the play.

It opens in the sales area of Hobson's shoe shop. Alice and Vickey reveal the problems they are having with their father, who drinks heavily. Albert, Alice's young man, comes to visit her, but is instead sold a pair of boots by Maggie, their elder sister, and departs greatly discomfited.

The brief conversation that follows between Maggie and Alice highlights their differing attitudes to love and marriage, and points to some of the pressures on Maggie because of her age.

The arrival of Hobson provides an opportunity for him to complain of the 'bumptiousness' of Alice and Vickey and inform us that, their mother being dead, he is having difficulty in forcing them to behave as he wants. His speeches show him as a blustering, self-opinionated bully. He bemoans the fact that his daughters cost him money, but swiftly changes the subject to dresses and fashion when Maggie asks him how much he gives them for their work in his shop. He threatens to marry off Alice and Vickey to men of his choosing, and in an insensitive and bruising comment, dismisses any chance of Maggie ever getting married.

The arrival of a customer, Mrs Hepworth, causes Hobson to stay in the shop. Her demand to see the person who made her shoes worries Hobson, who thinks she has come to complain. Her request allows the audience its first glimpse of Tubby Wadlow, and then a slightly longer glimpse of Willie Mossop. Having already demonstrated Maggie's skill as a saleswoman, this short scene confirms Willie as a craftsman. The audience has thus been prepared for the good sense of a business partnership between them. Mrs Hepworth's action of giving her card to Willie and demanding he should let her know his whereabouts should he move, prepares the ground for Maggie and Willie setting up in business.

The departure of Mrs Hepworth and the arrival of Jim Heeler, a friend of Hobson, is the signal for the girls to depart and for Hobson to unburden himself to his friend. He would like to get rid of two of his daughters, but on discovering this would cost money he changes his mind. His other daughter, Maggie, he wants to keep as she makes him money.

With Hobson and Heeler gone, Maggie and Willie are left together. Maggie proposes a partnership of both business and marriage. Whilst Willie does not actually refuse, he brings up the matter of his engagement to Ada, his landlady's daughter. On cue, Ada arrives, but is no competition for Maggie. It would seem Willie's engagement to her was a 'Hobson's Choice': he could not stand up to her mother. Willie refuses to seal his engagement to Maggie with a kiss, and scuttles back to his cellar.

Maggie's two sisters return, as does Hobson. The three of them are horrified at the engagement, and Hobson attempts to dismiss the matter out of hand. Maggie thwarts him in this respect, and ably defends her plans against his scorn. Hobson therefore calls Willie up from the cellar and attacks him with his belt. Willie's response is to stand up for himself and present Hobson with an ultimatum.

Act 2

The second act opens in the same place as the first, but it is now a very different atmosphere that prevails. It is marked by the inability of Alice, Vickey, and Tubby to make decisions about the day-to-day running of the shop. Alice and Vickey are still unmarried, and seem likely to remain so. They blame Maggie for their situation, and on cue, she and Willie arrive at the shop, together with Freddy Beenstock.

Events now move swiftly. It is disclosed that Hobson is lying drunk in Beenstock's cellar. Maggie has swiftly hatched a plot to force him to provide a dowry for each of Alice and Vickey, together with his permission for them to marry – under the threat of being sued for trespass.

The views of Alice and Vickey about aspects of getting married are disclosed, as a result of which Maggie feels free to remove some old furniture from the house. Albert is persuaded to push a hand-cart through the streets, much to his and Alice's annoyance.

The whole party goes off to Willie and Maggie's marriage, leaving Tubby in charge of the shop.

Act 3

The scene moves to the cellar at Oldfield Road where Willie and Maggie are setting up home and business. It is disclosed that Willie is learning to read and write.

Maggie has to fend off a number of questions as to where she and Willie got the finance to start off on their own. Before they leave the wedding feast, Albert and Freddy are persuaded to help with the washing up. Willie, nervous at the prospect of his wedding night, tries unsuccessfully to persuade the two men to stay a bit longer.

Hobson arrives, looking for Maggie's help with the writ he has found pinned to his chest. Maggie insists that it is Willie he should talk to, though eventually she does most of the talking. It is an amusing episode when Willie points out, in a very friendly and helpful way, the problems a writ would cause Hobson.

Maggie suggests the matter should be settled out of court, and then produces Albert to do the negotiating. He, along with Freddy, Alice and Vickey have been hiding in Maggie's bedroom. After some haggling, Hobson agrees to pay five hundred pounds damages. To his dismay he discovers he has been tricked, and that the money will be used as a dowry to enable Alice and Vickey to get married. Angrily, he storms off, leaving his daughters triumphant, and seemingly reconciled to each other.

Act 4

The scene is Hobson's living room. Tubby is seen attempting to prepare a bacon breakfast. Jim Heeler arrives, and we discover that Hobson is ill and has sent for the Doctor.

The Doctor arrives, and after a brief encounter with Jim, the latter is told to go. The Doctor pronounces Hobson very ill with alcoholic poisoning. He recommends, amongst other things, that Maggie should return home to look after him.

With the arrival of Maggie, called in by Tubby, the Doctor departs, confident that Hobson will be in good hands. Alice and Vickey arrive, and they both refuse to have a hand in looking after their father. Alice already has a house in a select part of town, and Vickey is expecting a baby. It is clear that, regardless of their commitments, they are determined never to return home, no matter how ill their father is. Furious at their attitude, Hobson congratulates Willie, whom Maggie sent for, for telling them their presence is not needed.

Hobson offers to allow Willie and Maggie back, under virtually the same régime as before. Willie refuses and offers a partnership deal, in which Hobson will be the 'sleeping partner'. Presented with no alternative, Hobson has to accept, and is meekly led off to the solicitor's office. Maggie and Willie have one final brief moment on stage together, when the audience can see that both their partnerships, marriage and business, are successful and certain to prosper.

Coursework and preparing for the examination

If you wish to gain a certificate in English literature then there is no substitute for studying the text/s on which you are to be examined. If you cannot be bothered to do that, then neither this guide nor any other will be of use to you.

Here we give advice on studying the text, writing a good essay, producing coursework, and sitting the examination. However, if you meet problems you should ask your teacher for help.

Studying the text

No, not just read – study. You must read your text at least twice. Do not dismiss it if you find a first reading difficult or uninteresting. Approach the text with an open mind and you will often find a second reading more enjoyable. When you become a more experienced reader enjoyment usually follows from a close study of the text, when you begin to appreciate both what the author is saying and the skill with which it is said.

Having read the text, you must now study it. We restrict our remarks here to novels and plays, though much of what is said can also be applied to poetry.

1 You will know in full detail all the major incidents in your text, **why**, **where** and **when** they happen, **who** is involved, **what** leads up to them and what follows.

2 You must show that you have an **understanding of the story**, the **characters**, and the **main ideas** which the author is exploring.

3 In a play you must know what happens in each act, and more specifically the organization of the scene structure – how one follows from and builds upon another. Dialogue in both plays and novels is crucial. You must have a detailed knowledge of the major dialogues and soliloquies and the part they play in the development of plot, and the development and drawing of character.

4 When you write about a novel you will not normally be expected to quote or to refer to specific lines but references to incidents and characters must be given, and they must be accurate and specific.

5 In writing about a play you will be expected both to paraphrase dialogue and quote specific lines, always provided, of course, that they are actually contributing something to your essay!

To gain full marks in coursework and/or in an examination you will also be expected to show your own reaction to, and appreciation of, the text studied. The teacher or examiner always welcomes those essays which demonstrate the student's own thoughtful response to the text. Indeed, questions often specify such a requirement, so do participate in those classroom discussions, the debates, class dramatizations of all or selected parts of your text, and the many other activities which enable a class to share and grow in their understanding and feeling for literature.

Making notes
A half-hearted reading of your text, or watching the 'film of the book' will not give you the necessary knowledge to meet the above demands.

As you study the text jot down sequences of events; quotations of note; which events precede and follow the part you are studying; the characters involved; what the part being studied contributes to the plot and your understanding of character and ideas.

Write single words, phrases and short sentences which can be quickly reviewed and which will help you to gain a clear picture of the incident being studied. Make your notes neat and orderly, with headings to indicate chapter, scene, page, incident, character, etc, so that you can quickly find the relevant notes or part of the text when revising.

Writing the essay

Good essays are like good books, in miniature; they are thought about, planned, logically structured, paragraphed, have a clearly defined pattern and development of thought, and are presented clearly – and with neat writing! All of this will be to no avail if the tools you use, i.e. words, and the skill with which you put them together to form your sentences and paragraphs are severely limited.

How good is your general and literary vocabulary? Do you understand and can you make appropriate use of such terms as 'soliloquy', 'character', 'plot', 'mood', 'dramatically effective', 'comedy', 'allusion', 'humour', 'imagery', 'irony', 'paradox', 'anti-climax', 'tragedy'? These are all words which examiners have commented on as being misunderstood by students.

Do you understand 'metaphor', 'simile', 'alliteration'? Can you say what their effect is on you, the reader, and how they enable the author to express himself more effectively than by the use of a different literary device? If you cannot, you are employing your time ineffectively by using them.

You are writing an English literature essay and your writing should be literate and appropriate. Slang, colloquialisms and careless use of words are not tolerated in such essays.

Essays for coursework

The exact number of essays you will have to produce and their length will vary; it depends upon the requirements of the examination board whose course you are following, and whether you will be judged solely on coursework or on a mixture of coursework and examination.

As a guide, however your course is structured, you will be required to provide a folder containing at least ten essays, and from that folder approximately five will be selected for moderation purposes. Of those essays, one will normally have been done in class-time under conditions similar to those of an examination. The essays must cover the complete range of course requirements and be the unaided work of the student. One board specifies that these pieces of continuous writing should be a minimum of 400 words long, and another, a minimum of 500 words long. Ensure that you know what is required for your course, and do not aim for the minimum amount – write a full essay then prune it down if necessary.

Do take care over the presentation of your final folder of coursework. There are many devices on the market which will enable you to bind your work neatly, and in such a way that you can easily insert new pieces. Include a 'Contents' page and a front and back cover to keep your work clean. Ring binders are unsuitable items to hand in for **final** assessment purposes as they are much too bulky.

What sort of coursework essays will you be set? All boards lay down criteria similar to the following for the range of student response to literature that the coursework must cover.

Work must demonstrate that the student:

1 shows an understanding not only of surface meaning but also of a deeper awareness of themes and attitudes;

2 recognizes and appreciates ways in which authors use language;

3 recognizes and appreciates ways in which writers achieve their effects, particularly in how the work is structured and in its characterization;

4 can write imaginatively in exploring and developing ideas so as to communicate a sensitive and informed personal response to what is read.

Much of what is said in the section **'Writing essays in an examination'** (below) is relevant here, but for coursework essays you have the advantage of plenty of time to prepare your work – so make use of it.

There is no substitute for arguing, discussing and talking about a question on a particular text or theme. Your teacher should give you plenty of opportunity for this in the classroom. Listening to what others say about a subject often opens up for you new ways to look at and respond to it. The same can be said for reading about a topic. Be careful not to copy down slavishly what others say and write. Jot down notes, then go away and think about what you have heard, read and written. Make more notes of your own and then start to clarify your own thoughts, feelings and emotions on the subject about which you are writing. Most students make the mistake of doing their coursework essays in a rush – you have time, so use it.

Take a great deal of care in planning your work. From all your notes, write a rough draft and then start the task of really perfecting it.

1 Look at your arrangement of paragraphs – is there a logical development of thought or argument? Do the paragraphs need rearranging in order? Does the first or last sentence of any paragraph need redrafting in order to provide a sensible link with the preceding or next paragraph?

2 Look at the pattern of sentences within each paragraph. Are your thoughts and ideas clearly developed and expressed? Have you used any quotations, paraphrases, or references to incidents to support your opinions and ideas? Are those references relevant and apt, or just 'padding'?

3 Look at the words you have used. Try to avoid repeating words in close proximity one to another. Are the words you have used to comment on the text being studied the most appropriate and effective, or just the first ones you thought of?

4 Check your spelling and punctuation.

5 Now write a final draft, the quality of which should reflect the above considerations.

Writing essays in an examination
Read the question. Identify the key words and phrases. Write them down, and as they are dealt with in your essay plan, tick them off.

Plan your essay. Spend about five minutes jotting down ideas; organize your thoughts and ideas into a logical and developing order – a structure is essential to the production of a good essay. Remember, brief, essential notes only!

Write your essay
How long should it be? There is no magic length. What you must do is answer the question set, fully and sensitively in the time allowed. You will probably have about forty minutes to answer an essay question, and within that time you should produce an essay between roughly 350 and 500 words in length. Very short answers will not do justice to the question, very long answers will probably contain much irrelevant information and waste time that should be spent on the next answer.

How much quotation? Use only that which is apt and contributes to the clarity and quality of your answer. No examiner will be impressed by 'padding'.

What will the examiners be looking for in an essay?
1 An answer to the question set, and not a prepared answer to another, albeit slightly similar, question done in class.

2 A well-planned, logically structured and paragraphed essay with a beginning, middle and end.

3 Accurate references to plot, character, theme, as required by the question.

4 Appropriate, brief, and if needed, frequent quotation and references to support and demonstrate the comments that you are making in your essay.

5 Evidence that reading the text has prompted in you a personal response to it, as well as some judgment and appreciation of its literary merit.

How do you prepare to do this?
1 During your course you should write between three to five essays on each text.

2 Make good use of class discussion etc, as mentioned in a previous paragraph on page 73.

3 Try to see a live performance of a play. It may help to see a film of a play or book, though be aware that directors sometimes leave out episodes, change their order, or worse, add episodes that are not in the original – so be very careful. In the end, there is no substitute for **reading and studying** the text!

Try the following exercises without referring to any notes or text.

1 Pick a character from your text.

2 Make a list of his/her qualities – both positive and negative ones, or aspects that you cannot quite define. Jot down single words to describe each quality. If you do not know the word you want, use a thesaurus, but use it in conjunction with a dictionary and make sure you are fully aware of the meaning of each word you use.

3 Write a short sentence which identifies one or more places in the text where you think each quality is demonstrated.

4 Jot down any brief quotation, paraphrase of conversation or outline of an incident which shows that quality.

5 Organize the list. Identify groupings which contrast the positive and negative aspects of the character.

6 Write a description of that character which makes full use of the material you have just prepared.

7 What do you think of the character you have just described? How has he/she reacted to and coped with the pressures of the other characters, incidents, and the setting of the story? Has he/she changed in any way? In no more than 100 words, including 'evidence' taken from the text, write a balanced assessment of the character, and draw some conclusions.

You should be able to do the above without notes, and without the text, unless you are to take an examination which allows the use of plain texts. In plain text examinations you are allowed to take in a copy of your text. It must be without notes, either your own or the publisher's. The intention is to enable you to consult a text in the examination so as to confirm memory of detail, thus enabling a candidate to quote and refer more accurately in order to illustrate his/her views much more effectively. Examiners will expect a high standard of accurate reference, quotation and comment in a plain text examination.

Sitting the examination

You will have typically between two and five essays to write and you will have roughly 40 minutes, on average, to write each essay.

On each book you have studied, you should have a choice of doing at least one out of two or three essay titles set.

1   **Before sitting the exam**, make sure you are completely clear in your mind that you know exactly how many questions you must answer, which sections of the paper you must tackle, and how many questions you may, or must, attempt on any one book or in any one section of the paper. If you are not sure, ask your teacher.

2   **Always read the instructions** given at the top of your examination paper. They are

there to help you. Take your time, and try to relax – panicking will not help.

3 **Be very clear about timing, and organizing your time.**

(a) Know how long the examination is.
(b) Know how many questions you must do.
(c) Divide (b) into (a) to work out how long you may spend on each question. (Bear in mind that some questions may attract more marks, and should therefore take proportionately more time.)
(d) Keep an eye on the time, and do not spend more than you have allowed for any one question.
(e) If you have spare time at the end you can come back to a question and do more work on it.
(f) Do not be afraid to jot down notes as an aid to memory, but do cross them out carefully after use – a single line will do!

4 **Do not rush the decision** as to which question you are going to answer on a particular text.

(a) Study each question carefully.
(b) Be absolutely sure what each one is asking for.
(c) Make your decision as to which you will answer.

5 **Having decided which question** you will attempt:

(a) jot down the key points of the actual question – use single words or short phrases;
(b) think about how you are going to arrange your answer. Five minutes here, with some notes jotted down, will pay dividends later;
(c) write your essay, and keep an eye on the time!

6 **Adopt the same approach** for all questions. Do write answers for the maximum number of questions you are told to attempt. One left out will lose its proportion of the total marks. Remember also, you will never be awarded extra marks, over and above those already allocated, if you write an extra long essay on a particular question.

7 **Do not waste time** on the following:

(a) an extra question – you will get no marks for it;
(b) worrying about how much anyone else is writing, they can't help you!
(c) relaxing at the end with time to spare – you do not have any. Work up to the very moment the invigilator tells you to stop writing. Check and recheck your work, including spelling and punctuation. Every single mark you gain helps, and that last mark might tip the balance between success and failure – the line has to be drawn somewhere.

8 **Help the examiner.**

(a) Do not use red or green pen or pencil on your paper. Examiners usually annotate your script in red and green, and if you use the same colours it will cause unnecessary confusion.
(b) Leave some space between each answer or section of an answer. This could also help you if you remember something you wish to add to your answer when you are checking it.
(c) Number your answers as instructed. If it is question 3 you are doing, do not label it 'C'.
(d) Write neatly. It will help you to communicate effectively with the examiner who is trying to read your script.

Glossary of literary terms

Mere knowledge of the words in this list or other specialist words used when studying literature is not sufficient. You must know when to use a particular term, and be able to describe what it contributes to that part of the work which is being discussed.

For example, merely to label something as being a metaphor does not help an examiner or teacher to assess your response to the work being studied. You must go on to analyse what the literary device contributes to the work. Why did the author use a metaphor at all? Why not some other literary device? What extra sense of feeling or meaning does the metaphor convey to the reader? How effective is it in supporting the author's intention? What was the author's intention, as far as you can judge, in using that metaphor?

Whenever you use a particular literary term you must do so with a purpose and that purpose usually involves an explanation and expansion upon its use. Occasionally you will simply use a literary term 'in passing', as, for example, when you refer to the 'narrator' of a story as opposed to the 'author' – they are not always the same! So please be sure that you understand both the meaning and purpose of each literary term you employ.

This list includes only those words which we feel will assist in helping you to understand the major concepts in play and novel construction. It makes no attempt to be comprehensive. These are the concepts which examiners frequently comment upon as being inadequately grasped by many students. Your teacher will no doubt expand upon this list and introduce you to other literary devices and words within the context of the particular work/s you are studying – the most useful place to experience and explore them and their uses.

Plot This is the plan or story of a play or novel. Just as a body has a skeleton to hold it together, so the plot forms the 'bare bones' of the work of literature in play or novel form. It is however, much more than this. It is arranged in time, so one of the things which encourages us to continue reading is to see what happens next. It deals with causality, that is how one event or incident causes another. It has a sequence, so that in general, we move from the beginning through to the end.

Structure The arrangement and interrelationship of parts in a play or novel are obviously bound up with the plot. An examination of how the author has structured his work will lead us to consider the function of, say, the 43 letters which are such an important part of *Pride and Prejudice*. We would consider the arrangement of the time-sequence in *Wuthering Heights* with its 'flashbacks' and their association with the different narrators of the story. In a play we would look at the scene divisions and how different events are placed in a relationship so as to produce a particular effect; where soliloquies occur so as to inform the audience of a character's innermost emotions and feelings. Do be aware that great works of fiction are not just simply thrown together by their authors. We study a work in detail, admiring its parts and the intricacies of its structure. The reason for a work's greatness has to do with the genius of its author and the care of its construction. Ultimately, though, we do well to remember that it is the work as a whole that we have to judge, not just the parts which make up that whole.

Narrator   A narrator tells or relates a story. In *Wuthering Heights* various characters take on the task of narrating the events of the story: Cathy, Heathcliff, etc, as well as being, at other times, central characters taking their part in the story. Sometimes the author will be there, as it were, in person, relating and explaining events. The method adopted in telling the story relates very closely to style and structure.

Style   The manner in which something is expressed or performed, considered as separate from its intrinsic content or meaning. It might well be that a lyrical, almost poetical style will be used, for example concentrating on the beauties and contrasts of the natural world as a foil to the narration of the story and creating emotions in the reader which serve to heighten reactions to the events being played out on the page. It might be that the author uses a terse, almost staccato approach to the conveyance of his story. There is no simple route to grasping the variations of style which are to be found between different authors or indeed within one novel. The surest way to appreciate this difference is to read widely and thoughtfully and to analyse and appreciate the various strategies which an author uses to command our attention.

Character   A person represented in a play or story. However, the word also refers to the combination of traits and qualities distinguishing the individual nature of a person or thing. Thus, a characteristic is one such distinguishing quality: in *Pride and Prejudice*, the pride and prejudices of various characters are central to the novel, and these characteristics which are associated with Mr Darcy, Elizabeth, and Lady Catherine in that novel, enable us to begin assessing how a character is reacting to the surrounding events and people. Equally, the lack of a particular trait or characteristic can also tell us much about a character.

Character development   In *Pride and Prejudice*, the extent to which Darcy's pride or Elizabeth's prejudice is altered, the recognition by those characters of such change, and the events of the novel which bring about the changes, are central to any exploration of how a character develops, for better or worse.

Irony   This is normally taken to be the humorous or mildly sarcastic use of words to imply the opposite of what they say. It also refers to situations and events and thus you will come across references such as prophetic, tragic, and dramatic irony.

Dramatic irony   This occurs when the implications of a situation or speech are understood by the audience but not by all or some of the characters in the play or novel. We also class as ironic words spoken innocently but which a later event proves either to have been mistaken or to have prophesied that event. When we read in the play *Macbeth*:

> *Macbeth*
> Tonight we hold a solemn supper, sir,
> And I'll request your presence.

> *Banquo*
> Let your highness
> Command upon me, to the which my duties
> Are with a most indissoluble tie
> Forever knit.

we, as the audience, will shortly have revealed to us the irony of Macbeth's words. He does not expect Banquo to attend the supper as he plans to have Banquo murdered before the supper occurs. However, what Macbeth does not know is the prophetic irony of Banquo's response. His 'duties. . . a most indissoluble tie' will be fulfilled by his appearance at the supper as a ghost – something Macbeth certainly did not forsee or welcome, and which Banquo most certainly did not have in mind!

Tragedy   This is usually applied to a play in which the main character, usually a person of importance and outstanding personal qualities, falls to disaster through the combination of personal failing and circumstances with which he cannot deal. Such tragic happenings may also be central to a novel. In *The Mayor of Casterbridge*, flaws in Henchard's character are partly responsible for his downfall and eventual death.

In Shakespeare's plays *Macbeth* and *Othello*, the tragic heroes from which the two plays take their names are both highly respected and honoured men who have proven their outstanding personal qualities. Macbeth, driven on by his ambition and that of his very determined wife, kills his king. It leads to civil war in his country, to his own eventual downfall and death, and to his wife's suicide. Othello, driven to an insane jealousy by the cunning of his lieutenant, Iago, murders his own innocent wife and commits suicide.

Satire Where topical issues, folly or evil are held up to scorn by means of ridicule and irony – the satire may be subtle or openly abusive.

In *Animal Farm*, George Orwell used the rebellion of the animals against their oppressive owner to satirize the excesses of the Russian revolution at the beginning of the 20th century. It would be a mistake, however, to see the satire as applicable only to that event. There is a much wider application of that satire to political and social happenings both before and since the Russian revolution and in all parts of the world.

Images An image is a mental representation or picture. One that constantly recurs in *Macbeth* is clothing, sometimes through double meanings of words: 'he seems rapt withal', 'Why do you dress me in borrowed robes?', 'look how our partner's rapt', 'Like our strange garments, cleave not to their mould', 'Whiles I stood rapt in the wonder of it', 'which would be worn now in their newest gloss', 'Was the hope drunk Wherein you dressed yourself?', 'Lest our old robes sit easier than our new.', 'like a giant's robe upon a dwarfish thief'. All these images serve to highlight and comment upon aspects of Macbeth's behaviour and character. In Act 5, Macbeth the loyal soldier who was so honoured by his king at the start of the play, struggles to regain some small shred of his self-respect. Three times he calls to Seyton for his armour, and finally moves toward his destiny with the words 'Blow wind, come wrack, At least we'll die with harness on our back' – his own armour, not the borrowed robes of a king he murdered.

Do remember that knowing a list of images is not sufficient. You must be able to interpret them and comment upon the contribution they make to the story being told.

Theme A unifying idea, image or motif, repeated or developed throughout a work.

In *Pride and Prejudice*, a major theme is marriage. During the course of the novel we are shown various views of and attitudes towards marriage. We actually witness the relationships of four different couples through their courtship, engagement and eventual marriage. Through those events and the examples presented to us in the novel of other already married couples, the author engages in a thorough exploration of the theme.

This list is necessarily short. There are whole books devoted to the explanation of literary terms. Some concepts, like style, need to be experienced and discussed in a group setting with plenty of examples in front of you. Others, such as dramatic irony, need keen observation from the student and a close knowledge of the text to appreciate their significance and existence. All such specialist terms are well worth knowing. But they should be used only if they enable you to more effectively express your knowledge and appreciation of the work being studied.

Titles in the series

A level

Coriolanus   The Pardoner's Tale

GCSE

Animal Farm   Macbeth
The Crucible   A Man for All Seasons
Far from the Madding Crowd   The Mayor of Casterbridge
Great Expectations   Of Mice and Men
Hobson's Choice   Pride and Prejudice
An Inspector Calls   Pygmalion
Jane Eyre   Romeo and Juliet
Lord of the Flies   To Kill A Mockingbird